Praise for

REAL CHANGE

"*Real Change* is a real gift to us all at a crucial time in our human evolution, helping us cultivate the clarity to bring deeply needed transformation into our personal and public lives."

—Dan Siegel, *New York Times* bestselling author of
Brainstorm, The Whole-Brain Child, and *No-Drama Discipline*

"Salzberg's wisdom is a compass. Her teaching helps readers navigate through unnerving times, serves as a salve for fractured hearts, and illustrates who we can be personally and collectively if we allow ourselves to embrace compassion as a path to clarity."

—Jamia Wilson, director and publisher of
Feminist Press, author, and activist

"In this book, Sharon has bridged the worlds of mindfulness and social action. The self-inquiry tools she gives us can be used by everyone involved in social change, from philanthropists to leaders in corporations, foundations, and governments."

—Jeffrey C. Walker, chairman of New Profit

"Sharon Salzberg is a gift to the world of mindfulness and a leader amongst meditators; her timeless wisdom has helped countless people reclaim their power." —Yung Pueblo, author of *Inward*

"Sharon's true strength—as both one of the greatest spiritual teachers of our time, and as a great writer—is mixing her own insights with the wisdom narratives of others. In this book she does just that."

—Ethan Nichtern, author of *The Road Home:
A Contemporary Exploration of the Buddhist Path*

"Sharon Salzberg's depth of wisdom and openhearted kindness gets better and better book after book!"

—Robert A. F. Thurman, author of *Man of Peace:
The Illustrated Life Story of the Dalai Lama of Tibet*

ALSO BY SHARON SALZBERG

Real Love:
The Art of Mindful Connection

Real Happiness at Work:
Meditations for Accomplishment, Achievement, and Peace

The Kindness Handbook:
A Practical Companion

Love Your Enemies:
How to Break the Anger Habit & Be a Whole Lot Happier
(with Robert Thurman)

Real Happiness:
The Power of Meditation

The Force of Kindness:
Change Your Life with Love and Compassion

Lovingkindness:
The Revolutionary Art of Happiness

Faith:
Trusting Your Own Deepest Experience

Insight Meditation:
A Step-by-Step Course on How to Meditate
(with Joseph Goldstein)

A Heart as Wide as the World

REAL CHANGE

MINDFULNESS
TO HEAL
OURSELVES AND
THE WORLD

*

SHARON SALZBERG

FLATIRON
BOOKS
NEW YORK

www.flatironbooks.com

Library of Congress Cataloging-in-Publication Data

Names: Salzberg, Sharon, author.
Title: Real change : mindfulness to heal ourselves and the world / Sharon Salzberg.
Description: First Edition. | New York : Flatiron Books, 2020. | Includes index.
Identifiers: LCCN 2020001229 | ISBN 9781250310576 (hardcover) |
    ISBN 9781250310583 (ebook)
Subjects: LCSH: Mindfulness (Psychology) | Self-actualization (Psychology) |
    Social change—Psychological aspects.
Classification: LCC BF637.M56 S285 2020 | DDC 158.1/3—dc23
LC record available at https://lccn.loc.gov/2020001229

Our books may be purchased in bulk for promotional, educational, or business
use. Please contact your local bookseller or the Macmillan Corporate and
Premium Sales Department at 1-800-221-7945, extension 5442, or by email at
MacmillanSpecialMarkets@macmillan.com.

First Edition: 2020

10 9 8 7 6 5 4 3 2 1

CONTENTS

✳

PREFACE   vii

Introduction: We Are All in This Together   1
1. Change Is Possible   7
2. Agency   30
3. Awakening to the Fire: When Anger Turns to Courage   53
4. Grief to Resilience   79
5. Coming Home to Ourselves   109
6. Interconnectedness   137
7. Seeing More Clearly   169
8. Exquisite Balance   193

GRATEFUL ACKNOWLEDGMENTS   223
INDEX   225

PREFACE

✳

Wisdom for Our Time and All Time

I've been working on this book for a long time and finished it just before the massive disruption, harm, and anxiety wrought by COVID-19 was made manifest. It was written before the inequities, prejudice, shortsightedness, and fear that form the scaffolding of several of society's structures were so powerfully highlighted. It was written before so many of the things we casually expected for tomorrow or next week or next month were turned right around on their heads.

In these times of great loss and uncertainty, we each look for what can sustain us, what can help provide assurance that something is intact. We look for something essential that has not been blown apart, and we yearn to once again align with our deepest values, so we can find renewal.

After an atomic bomb blasted Hiroshima in 1945, further panic swept through the city when rumors arose that grass, trees, and flowers would never grow there again. Was this disaster of such proportions that everything people had relied on, everything they had cherished, the very laws of nature, had exploded along with the bomb? Although, when faced with such intense suffering, we may certainly question whether there is any underlying possibility of renewal, of authenticity, of goodness, the grass actually did grow once more in Hiroshima.

Seeing that, despite having also seen their world suddenly, brutally blown apart, survivors were more able to go on. Reflecting on this story, I am reminded to look for what is whole, integrated, undamaged, even in the face of devastation or loss.

One of the original meanings of the Sanskrit word *dharma*—often translated as "the way of things" or "the law of nature"—is "that which can uphold us, that which can support us." As the conditions of the pandemic unfolded, and I looked for what could support me as I grappled with the fundamental question—"What's still true?"—I turned once again to timeless wisdom, and time-tested methods of meditation.

I have asked myself that potent question repeatedly. It always reminds me to look deeply—within myself and outside of myself as well: "What's still true?"

In that light, I've been examining some familiar images and metaphors. For example, to create audio recordings, I was reading aloud some of the guided meditations you'll find in this book. Among these was a lovingkindness meditation where we offer a sense of care and inclusion to a sequence of different kinds of people. One of the classical categories of recipients is someone known as a "neutral person," someone we don't generally like or dislike—the kind of person we tend to overlook or discount, not through bias or antipathy, but mostly through sheer indifference.

It's suggested that you choose someone you tend to see now and then, just so you can gauge the feeling of connection you might find growing toward them. For more than thirty years my colleagues and I have commonly recommended someone like a supermarket checkout clerk as a neutral person: the very epitome of someone who performs a service for us but whom we tend to be conditioned to disregard. As I was reading the instruction aloud, in the midst of the pandemic and social distancing, I was dumbfounded. *We wouldn't be eating if these people were not showing up for work*, I thought. *It makes no sense to have so much indifference toward such people!*

I know these shifts and revelations are good to wake up to, even if they can leave us somewhat unsettled. Frequently we find a previously overlooked truth, like, "Look at that! I am actually dependent on all kinds of people that I might have tended to objectify, as though they weren't people with hopes and dreams and fears and problems just like me." I think it's imperative to look now not just at what we're used to, but at the deepest places within us and between us to consider, "What's still true?"

As I was reading this book yet one more time, in light of current events, I was moved by a sense of greater peace and conviction, believing that the grass and flowers could grow again after devastation, that there was a way to reclaim wholeness and abide in integrity. The path laid out in this book seemed to me to be as true as it ever was for our personal healing and our ability to affect the world: feeling the stirring of agency; transforming anger to courage; moving from grief to resilience; allowing joy; taking care of ourselves as well as one another; living by the truth of interconnection and the power of compassion. This is a book not only about trying to bring about change in the world, but also about how this ever-changing world also changes us in the process.

May this book be of benefit, may it help to ease suffering, and serve to connect us further so that we are not defined by isolation and fear, but rather by wisdom, generosity, and love.

INTRODUCTION

✳

We Are All in This Together

FROM THE TIME I FIRST heard the Buddha's view on the innate dignity and worth of all, I thought it was just breathtaking. Not only was it personally transforming for me, helping me feel I finally belonged, that I was a part of a bigger picture of life, but I quickly saw the implications of such a perspective on how one might choose to act in the world.

Mindfulness and even lovingkindness meditation practices are commonly thought of as personal and inward-focused, but they can very much be social practices as well. When we get in touch with our own pain or the pain of others, meditation is not just a salve; it can provide the impetus to work for change. The engagement that results can be an openhearted demonstration of what we care about most deeply.

Efforts toward change are an expression of our own innate dignity and testament to the belief that what we do matters in this world. We engage not only to try to foster change right now, we engage to enliven what we believe to someday yet be possible.

Robert Thurman, a professor at Columbia University, uses an image to teach how anyone can practice living with compassion. "Imagine you're on the New York City subway," he says, "and these extraterrestrials come and zap the subway car so that all of you in it are going to be together forever." If someone is hungry on the subway car, we help get them food. If someone begins to panic, we do our best to calm them down. Not because we necessarily like them or approve of them but because we are going to be together forever. Well, Robert continues, guess what? The truth is that everyone on the subway car *is* in it together—we share this planet, we share this life, and our actions and reactions, and theirs, ripple out extensively.

We don't live in isolated silos, disconnected from everyone else—it just feels that way sometimes. What happens to others inevitably affects us. Even if we have been ignoring or unaware of the situation of those we don't know, we can wake up and see that our lives are actually intricately connected. What happens "over there" never nicely just stays "over there"—it flows out. And what we do over here matters. This interconnectedness is not only a spiritual realization—science shows us this, economics shows us this, environmental awareness certainly shows us this, and even epidemiology shows us this.

We all struggle with what to change and what to let be, what we can affect and what we can't, the effort it takes to foster change, and how it's all too possible to burn out or shut down. I've learned that meditation can provide tools to help courage grow out of rage and resilience out of grief. I've learned that if your own life has been shattered by the actions of others, the perspective meditation offers can help you become whole. And even though it runs counter to what many of us have been taught, I've learned that deep acceptance is not inertness.

Our times, and maybe all times, can seem aggressive and confounding, making many uncertain of what to think and wary of getting involved. Sometimes at the heart of this doubt is feeling overwhelmed by the immensity of woes around us. The act of voting, of standing alone in that booth marking off your choices, can seem so small and ineffectual. Volunteering in a soup kitchen can seem a meager effort in the face of homelessness and poverty and food insecurity. And yet, I don't see how apathy, cynicism, a perpetual sense of defeat, or armoring myself against caring is any better! What may be a small difference in our eyes can be a big difference for someone else whose life would be directly impacted.

I've been exploring these topics for decades now, both with people who ask for my help and in dealing with the challenges in my own life. *Real Change* is the book I've been wanting to write for years, to explore the intersection between the activity of working toward change in the world and the clarity and compassion arising from mindfulness and lovingkindness practice. The book is organized to map out the journey we often take toward a more impactful and sustainable expression of our values: expanding our vision; embodying real efforts toward change; working with the anger and grief that accompany a clear-eyed look at pain; supporting ourselves and remembering joy in the midst of challenging realities; looking afresh at who counts, who matters; awakening discernment and insight; coming to balance and knowing peace.

Included within the text are various meditation or contemplation exercises to try out. Each meditation is designed to encapsulate the thinking of the chapter and serves as a training in bringing those principles to life—by steadying our attention, focusing our energy, helping us let go more gracefully, and expanding our experience of love and compassion. To experiment with them, you might set aside ten minutes or so, sit comfortably, read the suggestions, then close your eyes if you feel at ease doing so (it's fine to keep them partially open), and try them out. Consider doing each exercise a number of times so that having tried a few of them and being more familiar with them, you can see if there are some you'd like to build into a habit.

For this book, I've spoken with many inspiring changemakers. From poets and playwrights to advocates for equal pay, social justice, environmental stewardship, and many more. Some practice meditation in a classical sense and some don't, but they all grapple with similar experiences and challenges in their quest to have a positive impact on the world.

Their work, their struggles and successes, so often connect, for me, to the teachings of mindfulness, lovingkindness, and the 2,500-year-old wisdom of the Buddha. I say that not because I am trying to proselytize the institution of Buddhism (which can fail to live up to its own values) but because the teachings and especially the practices offered by the Buddha changed my life, enabled me to see the power in wisdom and compassion, and are accessible to anyone regardless of faith, tradition, or belief.

These changemakers have generously allowed me to quote them in my efforts to convey how to navigate these waters of action and awareness in the healthiest ways possible. I want to share their insights and stories. We make this journey together.

1

CHANGE IS POSSIBLE

✳

IN THE TRADITION I'VE BEEN trained in, it's a long-standing custom to dedicate the positive energy arising from meditation practice to others. So, in the morning, before I meditate, I often spend time thinking of someone I know who is struggling. Naturally, the particular recipient can differ depending on who comes to mind on a given day. I might contemplate someone I met who is caring for a parent with Alzheimer's or a schoolchild I know trying to recover from a traumatic, violent experience. Perhaps I reflect on a community that is being throttled, as if their voices didn't count, or I might think of a horrific thing that happened just down the street—like the painting of swastikas on university walls.

Sometimes what captures my attention is the blatant cruelty described matter-of-factly in the news every day, as though the action reported were a normal way for people to treat one another. When I hear of someone being brutally treated, the action seems predicated on the assumption that the person being metaphorically or literally kicked is an object, like a piece of furniture, rather than a person with feelings and dreams and obligations and fears. Some mornings, I just want to go back to bed.

Recently, when I was doing this contemplation, instead of feeling inspired by dedicating the meditation, I just felt burdened, tired out by the relentless onslaught of pain everywhere I looked. I knew I needed a break, something to cradle my aching heart, to remind me of forces unseen and of a broad, open view of change. I had become frozen.

THE STRESS RESPONSE

MOST OF US are familiar with the description of the fight-or-flight response to stress or trauma: our common tendency to perceive a situation as an imminent threat, and react either by gearing up (physiologically, hormonally, and emotionally) to fight for survival or alternatively gearing up to run away as fast as we can.

I felt gratified when stress experts expanded these familiar descriptions to include another common, ready reaction: freezing. It made sense to me as soon as I heard it. We each engage in all three of these reactions, of course, but it seems like each of us has a tendency to gravitate toward one of these more than the others, based on our individual conditioning. I'll lay claim to freezing as my most frequent automatic reaction, rather than getting ready to bolt or starting to attack.

When we freeze, we're like the proverbial deer in the headlights. We try to disappear by declaring invisibility. I was recently playing peekaboo with a three-year-old who seemed convinced that I couldn't see her if she covered her own eyes. That reaction can be adaptive for a while: sometimes we really don't have the resources on the spot to fully process what is happening, and numbness or temporary dissociation buys us some needed time. It's no surprise, though, that freezing can also be greatly maladaptive. Some stress experts say fighting or fleeing are signs of hope, while freezing is lanced through with strands of hopelessness. Therefore, it can be harder to deal with.

Our reflexive responses of fighting, fleeing, or freezing—when faced with overly stressful situations or reliving trauma—can be qualitatively different from the marshaling of energy to strongly respond to a need. Our reflexive responses are often fitful and erratic, sending us lurching in reaction without a lot of clarity—more a cry of agony than a battle cry that recalls our purpose and brings us together with others in common cause. My own age-old habitual tendency to freeze, for example—numbing out, disassociating, spacing out, wanting to go to sleep—is not a useful place to stay long term if you really want to make a difference.

I wouldn't want to pathologize any of our common reactions to stress or trauma, however bad they might feel. The main tools I bring to this challenge of getting stuck in the face of fear are *mindfulness* and *lovingkindness* practices—which I have trained in and taught over the course of four decades. The point of developing these qualities is not to judge ourselves harshly when we are less than mindful or kind but to learn how to not be stuck in an automatic reaction. We practice in order to cultivate a sense of *agency*, to understand that a range of responses is open to us. We practice to remember to breathe, to have the space in the midst of adversity to recall our values, what we really care about—and to find support in our inner strength, and in one another.

Some threats are greatly exaggerated, of course, because of our anxiety, or our feelings of weakness or inadequacy, our entrenched certainty that we will be defeated. Some threats are not real; they live only in our imagination. And while some threats are quite real, we often see them as out of proportion to how dangerous they actually are, heightening our fear. In the times we live in now—when there is great division all around the world—people are often highlighting differences rather than similarities, alienation rather than interconnection. Hatred feels like it is surging, and the scaffolding that has held our communities up—the altruism taught by faith-based traditions, the commitment to good-heartedness in secular traditions, a vision of the body politic's common good—feels like it has become very shaky. On any given day, anywhere across the globe, people seem more readily torn apart than brought together.

THE ACHING HEART

THE REACTIONS OF fight, flight, or freeze appear to be more of a chronic state that is starting to rule our patterns of consumption and communication, our media, our use of technology, our relationships, the dimensions of our generosity, and the limits of our imagination. We are more afraid, and we are isolating ourselves more: not surprisingly, the number of people describing themselves as quite lonely is shooting up, as reported in the United States, in England, in Japan.

It's no wonder we're fearful and despairing, since many times these days it can feel like we're being hit with an avalanche of sad news on many days, while we so rarely hear inspiring visions of the future. Many people, particularly young people, feel trapped. They say that they find themselves participating in, and therefore perpetuating, a system they did not create, that does not reflect their values, and is destructive of the planet and inequitable. How to have inspiration, they ask, when the only game in town feels rigged? There's a cognitive dissonance that goes along with that kind of trapped feeling. It's a form of daily moral injury, what journalist Diane Silver described as a "soul wound that pierces a person's identity, sense of morality and relationship to society."

As I've traveled around the world teaching, I've gotten a sense of the prevalence and depth of the moral injury resulting from world events. In the political climate of the United States in early 2018, I myself encountered near at hand the very ingredients I needed to get agitated: deception from authority figures, shifting narratives not in accord with objective reality, one's own perception of the truth continually undermined. My childhood had been shaped by people who I believe cared deeply about me. Yet they thought the best way to express that caring was by never mentioning my mother after she died when I was nine. They thought it best to describe my father's overdose of sleeping pills when I was eleven as accidental—never explaining how a mere accident led to the rest of his life being spent in one psychiatric facility or another. It was painful to figure out when I was away at college: "Oh, that kind of pattern speaks more of suicidal intention than of an accident." Feeling something to be true right down to the cells of your body while having that truth affirmed exactly nowhere outside, in fact denied, can make you feel just crazy. That was the flavor of my childhood.

It strongly reminds me of anthropologist Gregory Bateson's double bind theory—a once popular (first put forth in the 1950s) though now discarded theory about the roots of schizophrenia. A double bind is exemplified by receiving two conflicting messages, so that successfully responding to one means you've failed in response to the other. (A common example is a mother telling you she loves you while her facial expression and body language communicate distaste.) You come to feel torn apart, frustrated, doubting yourself more and more. It might not be the source of schizophrenia, but it can be fearsome. As I looked for articles on this topic through Google, I saw one titled "The Double Bind Theory, Still Crazy-Making After All These Years."

In service of a more malicious intent to conceal, manipulate, or dominate, these double messages are tactics designed to frighten or confuse, fostering the repeated suggestion that you can't trust yourself or your perceptions and feelings. We call this *gaslighting*—a term originating with the 1944 Ingrid Bergman movie, *Gaslight*, and used colloquially since the 1960s to describe efforts to manipulate someone's perception of reality to the point that they question their sanity.

I knew that inner landscape of collapse and chaos very well. Though when it emerged in the political turmoil of 2018, it had been quite some time since it had surged that strongly or been so sustained. But now, unlike in my childhood, I had tools I had learned in meditation practice. I had values that served as a North Star in my life, such as a respect for myself and others and a commitment to balance. I had insight into ways of fostering resilience and could remind myself, with genuineness, of the crucial fact that I was not alone. I believed in the healing power of love. Helplessness no longer felt natural, the way things are meant to be, but a distortion I could address and did address.

No matter the times we are living in, it takes some determination to acknowledge our own vulnerabilities alongside the truth of discord, and bias, and exploitation, and climate degradation, and yet also see what might be the source of light, or connection, or freedom.

For a while, a friend and I had a pact to send each other one piece of good news a day. We were not alone in this pursuit: the AI-based Google Assistant recently added a feature that provides news in response to the prompt "Tell me something good"; *Mindful* magazine calls out acts of kindness in its Top of Mind section; *The New York Times* has a regular good news feature, *The Washington Post* has the Optimist, and the *Los Angeles Times* has a good news Twitter feed; groups like Solutions Journalism highlight ways people are trying to work out our problems; and sites like Upworthy and the Good News Network are filled with uplift.

My friend was very into tortoises and quite knowledgeable about them. Apparently, tortoises were doing pretty well as we neared the end of the second decade of the twenty-first century, because I got a lot of very positive tortoise news, day after day. For me, though, on some days, between stories of racism, and misogyny, and gender bias, and children separated from their parents, and a resurgence of anti-Semitism, and stories of greed ruling over decency and even common sense, and school/concert/church/synagogue/mosque/mall mass shootings, a reciprocal uplifting article was very hard to find.

A kaleidoscope would be an apt image for this torrent of news, for with a flick of the wrist and a change in perspective and some different elements brought in, the whole constructed world can shift. The 2018 mass shooting at Marjory Stoneman Douglas High School in Parkland, Florida, was an unspeakable tragedy, and it also brought the world a glimpse of the strength and clarity and compassion that lives within the next generation.

Sari Kaufman was a junior at Marjory Stoneman Douglas when a former student went on that shooting spree on Valentine's Day, killing seventeen students and staff and wounding seventeen others. Sari ran for her life and survived. Along with several other students, she became active immediately after the event, speaking locally and nationally about doing something about gun violence and taking a leading role in an anti-gun-violence march past the school. Those young voices roared. For Sari, the work has been uplifting, but it does not remove the pain, which is indisputably present. In an interview for this book, we spoke about Parkland's March for Our Lives, which she helped organize. She said:

> When we marched past our school, we had thirty-five thousand people just completely silent, which was insane. To keep that many people quiet, and passing the memorial and passing the building where it happened—just being in the spot where everything changed, where this movement was created, it was just really inspiring. We marched around our school and then came back to the park. It was a weird day because it was like, "Wow, look at what we just did," but at the same time it was, "We did this because of what happened." So it was kind of bittersweet. I didn't know what to feel because I was just so happy that after all this work it was a huge success, but at the same time, I lost one of my friends. If that didn't happen to us, we wouldn't have had to have the march.

Months later, in June 2018, people around the world felt for the twelve boys, ranging in age from eleven to sixteen, and their soccer coach who were stuck in a small dry spot in a deep, water-filled cave in Thailand. They spent eighteen days there before a heroic and dangerous rescue by trained divers. They survived without food, with limited oxygen, and with only water that dripped from stalactites. An early rescue attempt ended in tragedy when a Thai Navy SEAL lost his life trying to reach them. As horrific as it was, the tragedy also reminded us—as we learned the boys meditated to marshal strength for their ordeal—that we have startling capacities within us. We have our vulnerabilities, and we can be fragile. But we are also strong, resilient. We can bounce back.

Ekapol Chanthawong, the boys' twenty-five-year-old assistant coach who learned to meditate from his mother and regularly practices at a monastery, said about guiding the boys in mindfulness meditation, "I like to call it my *transportable tranquility*, because it goes with me wherever I go. I do not need to go outside or down the street or up the block to search for it. It's already within me, waiting for me to knock and enter. My mother, who quoted philosophers and visionaries, often shared a favorite passage, that 'Tranquility itself is not freedom from the storm but peace *within it*.'"

SOFT AND STRONG

WHEN I WANT to summon strength and power in the midst of awfulness and hate, I contemplate water. Our ideas of strength so often surround images of things that are hard—like rock or even a clenched fist. Perhaps that's why we think love doesn't include strength, just softness. We are thinking in only one dimension.

That's why I think of water, in all its manifestations. Look at the many ways we experience water: it trickles, spurts, floods, pours, streams, soaks, and shows itself in many more modes. All these convey evanescence, release, flow. They are all about *not being stuck.*

Water is flexible, taking the shape of whatever vessel it flows into. It's always interacting, changing, in motion, yet revealing continual patterns of connection. An incarnation of the water in the juicy piece of fruit you ate yesterday may have fallen as rain halfway around the world last year, nourished a flower offered to a beloved in India, or Cleveland, or Buenos Aires. It might have refreshed an elephant in the African savanna, misted the face of a koala in Australia, or fogged in a flight from the San Francisco airport to the consternation of the delayed passengers.

Water can be so expressive, a signal of our most heartfelt feelings. We cry tears of sorrow, tears of outrage, tears of gratitude, and tears of joy.

Water can be puzzling, seeming weak or ineffectual, yielding too much, not holding firm. And yet over time, water will carve its own pathway, even through rock. And yes, water freezes. But it also melts.

RADICAL PRACTICE

HUMAN BEINGS HAVE always found uplift and inspiration in metaphors, like water, but we also take inspiration from other people, and their strength and resiliency in the face of difficult circumstances—the ways in which they unfreeze themselves and make change. Not just in one way but in as many ways as water flows. I have been so moved by people I know who act in ways that seek change and who also tap into an inner strength—a way of being as well as a way of acting. They have helped me find the courage to go beyond freezing, as well.

The people I find deeply inspiring derive their sense of purpose, their vision, their resolve, from different sources: faith traditions, traumatic losses, a sense of oneness with all that they learned in their families or a propulsion away from the values their families lived by. Their efforts in the world have been bolstered by community, nature, music, poetry. For me, the core meditations of mindfulness and lovingkindness have most directly awakened the same values of compassion, inclusion, and understanding, and I have found them the most sustaining practices of all. I celebrate the qualities that emerge from meditation practices and encourage us all to develop these tools to whatever degree we find helpful, but I myself don't just draw inspiration from meditation practitioners. I want to lift up exemplary human qualities wherever I see them emerge, however people get there, because it is in recognizing those qualities that we remember what's possible for us.

How these qualities will manifest in our lives may vary quite widely. When I was first talking about this book to one of my friends, the groundbreaking feminist author bell hooks, she told me she doesn't use the term *social action*. I am well accustomed to the word parsing of Buddhist scholars, the excruciating care they take to differentiate one term from another, and the painstaking detail with which they will do that, but I've told bell I think she has them all beat. She has a point, though.

For her, she said, *social action* calls to mind overt protests, like marches and picketing, and that limits the range of effective responses one might have to the challenges of the world around us. I agree with her that the scope of possible action that can initiate change, that can move us to act in big and small ways, is far vaster than protests. She suggested *radical thinking*, or *radical practice*.

And I thought right away, *What about art?* which I consider a profoundly radical practice. Many historians give great weight to art and the world of ideas, not just politics, in assessing forces of social change. For example, in the late Tony Judt's award-winning history of the development of Europe after World War II, *Post-war*, he counts the aesthetic, intellectual, and cultural movements of the time as significant factors in shaping a new world from the ashes of the old. Ideas artfully expressed move the mind.

Singer-songwriter Rosanne Cash, at a talk at Yale University in 2019, described art as a medium for social change. "I always thought that if world peace happened, or if great movements in society happened that lifted us all up, it wouldn't happen because some politicians spoke to each other. It would happen because art and music changed people enough that they could speak their convictions and access their own feelings."

Rosanne went on, "All art and music is political," because through art we "develop compassion and empathy . . . and when you know that other people suffer, you want to do something about it."

While writing this book, I volunteered in Puerto Rico for an organization called Bajacu' Boricua, in collaboration with the Holistic Life Foundation of Baltimore. They brought together a teaching team, half from Puerto Rico and half from the international community, to explore meditation, music, and movement as modes of healing and expression. This coincided with playwright and actor Lin-Manuel Miranda bringing his enormous musical theater hit *Hamilton* to the island as part of an effort to help in the long-delayed recovery from Hurricane Maria, offering all proceeds to the Flamboyan Arts Fund his family helped start to support music, theater, visual arts, dance, literature, and youth arts education.

I loved *Hamilton,* and as have many creative works, it deeply moved me. I would suggest that playwrights—not to mention choreographers, cinematographers, composers, poets, and more—are often engaging in radical acts that go far beyond mere entertainment.

Lynn Nottage and Sarah Jones are both playwrights who use art as a form of "radical practice." Sarah views art as a motivating and disrupting force. She wrote to me:

> At our best, those of us who dare (or feel compelled) to sit down to a blank page and chisel away at an idea until it feels true enough to live its own life, or those who are able to harness a world in their minds and use it to fill a void in the world of cinema, hopefully we are a useful example to others—whether they're moved by the work itself or just the process of creating something, the emotional risk-taking and vulnerability.

Likewise, Lynn is inspired by what she calls "a form of activism and writing that incites change and invites people to think—invites small revolutions, whether those revolutions are tiny shifts in perspective or whether those revolutions are ones that force people to go outside of themselves and do something surprising or different." A play is not a fixed thing, she says. It is enacted in the moment. "No matter how many times I produce a play, it is never the same play, because it's completed by the audience and by the energy that's in that room."

MINDFULNESS IS NOT ONLY FOR MOUNTAINTOPS

I'VE SPENT THE last four decades working to help people cultivate the inner capacities of mindfulness and lovingkindness through meditation and other methods. I know meditation is sometimes seen as a purely internal and esoteric practice, deeply spiritual and with positive repercussions for the practitioner, but nonetheless quite separate from day-to-day life—a retreat from life's pains and struggles. We think of gurus on mountaintops and disciples cloistered away in ashrams and caves, living pure, almost disembodied existences.

More and more people use mindfulness and compassion practices these days, moved by their reported influence on the nitty-gritty hurdles of day-to-day life. I'm not sure how many of those people would assert that these methods affect more than themselves and their immediate circle. But I do know that the outcomes of lovingkindness and mindfulness meditation practices *can* be foundations for engaging in the world in large, bold ways that are also realistic and sustainable. In the face of struggles for social justice, for making the world a better place even when the times feel daunting, mindfulness and lovingkindness practices can help provide us with the tools we need to navigate the emotional and conceptual terrain that comes with seeking to make change.

Sometimes these practices are seen as promoting the opposite of a commitment to social change; they're regarded as a sort of soporific we can imbibe so that we can feel good no matter what's going on around us. We can half snooze through life rather than engage with the suffering of others, or even of ourselves. That view of a meditative life paints a fuzzy, sepia-toned picture, a parallel to the disconnected freeze effect in the collection of fight, flight, or freeze stress reactions. It all seems so vague! So removed! So . . . numb!

Bhikkhu Bodhi, an American born in New York City in 1944, was ordained as a Buddhist monk in Sri Lanka in late 1972. He lived in Sri Lanka for almost twenty-four years. For most of his monastic life, he pursued scholarship and translation, as well as practicing and teaching meditation. In the last decade or so, following his return to the United States in 2002, he has increasingly turned to activism, speaking out about hunger and climate change and girls' education, among other matters. Although he was politically active in his college years, once he became a monk, he felt working on himself and learning the legacy of the ancient tradition was most important. However, he said recently, "I came to feel and to believe that our way of interpreting and applying Buddhism has to adjust itself to the dominant ethos of the age in which we're living, and to the vital and crucial needs arising from the conditions under which we're living." In other words, he came to feel that the conditions of our time require a robust response that reflects our inner values writ large as we look at the legacy of our societies, our priorities, our choices.

The truth is, meditation would not be as meaningful for me at this time in my life if it were just about *me*. For my part, my experience practicing, studying, and teaching mindfulness and lovingkindness meditations is that they work to:

- *build a quality of resilience that can shore us up for the long haul;*

- *help clear our minds to make better choices, with strategies based on the values we want to live by;*
- *teach us how to be with feelings of loss or frustration or pain in a way that's healing and onward leading, instead of devastating;*
- *help us focus our energies more productively and relieve the exhaustion of finding too many battles to fight;*
- *join forces with others more effectively and harmoniously;*
- *transform how we see ourselves, those we work with, and those whose decisions and actions we work against; and*
- *lighten and open our hearts as we cultivate the power of connection.*

A METTA MINUTE

THESE PRACTICES ALSO help me remember what I most care about and allow me to keep going in the face of adversity or criticism. In late June 2018, for example, I helped coordinate a minute of metta (lovingkindness) for children being held in detention. These kids, some as young as under a year, had been separated from their parents who were seeking asylum at the U.S. border. Though asylum-seeking is considered a legal form of entry, our government representatives were treating it—in action and in rhetoric—as though it were a terrible crime for mothers or fathers to flee war, hunger, and domestic violence in search of a better life for their children.

Reading about and seeing videos of these frightened children, seeing their parents desperate to be reunited, simply broke my heart, so I publicized the minute of mindfulness through Twitter at #mettaminute.

Some people who responded were very positive, grateful for

a way to not feel so alone, to have a reminder that this heinous practice was ongoing and we couldn't afford to look the other way. Several wrote about how exhausted they were by their own outrage and felt they needed another way to respond that incorporated love.

Others urged me to stop leading the meditation and instead donate to an organization working directly with those families. (I already had donated.) Some chided me and gently tried to steer me toward other forms of action, instead of what they saw as a mollifying, self-soothing, self-serving exercise. A few were more strident than that, deriding me for wasting people's time, describing me as ineffectual and stupid, "as bad as the people who send thoughts and prayers after a mass shooting, instead of working on things like background checks for people buying guns."

I responded first with this tweet: "I offer metta (lovingkindness) to those in ICE detention centers to remind myself not to disconnect. And because I remember what it was like as a child to feel abandoned. It's so much less painful to look the other way, but this is vital."

How do we keep witnessing the pain, especially if it is so evocative of the most difficult times in our own lives?

After the more dismissive or angry tweets started arriving, I wrote again, "I would never suggest meditation, prayer, positive thoughts as a replacement for action. But I know I need to connect to something bigger, repeatedly, to have energy to keep acting."

How do you keep going in your efforts toward change, when immediate success is not in sight, when you're awfully tired, when you're frustrated? Do you have a refuge in something bigger than the current circumstance? Where can we connect to something larger than what's in our immediate experience, larger than the small-minded views the world may be pulling us toward? How can we remember to reside more often within this bigger vision?

I've had the good fortune to meet Shantel Walker, thirty-five, who has worked for Papa John's Pizza in Brooklyn for almost twenty years, enduring erratic hours and unlivable earnings. Finally, she got fed up and joined strikes and street protests that brought national attention to the plight of the nearly four million people working in the United States in the fast-food franchises that are American icons. In 2013, she joined Fight for $15—a nationwide movement that later succeeded in increasing the minimum wage in New York City and elsewhere. She continues to volunteer in off hours for Fast Food Justice and Fast Food Forward, non-profits that work for the betterment of fast-food workers. At one point, she lost her job for five months because of organizing, but she said no punishment is worse than the punishment of a wage you can't live on.

Shantel works day in, day out to serve people pizza, and she is also a visionary. In an interview for this book, she told me:

A lot of people don't get ahead in society because they are only worried about themselves. Sometimes, you've got to not worry about yourself so much. You've got to worry about mankind and humanity, you've got to think if we don't all do something today, what is tomorrow going to bring? If I can't live on what I'm making now, how will it be for these kids around here in the next five or ten years? Will it get any better if I just sit here worrying about my own situation alone?

Why are we doing what's wrong? Why are we listening to someone who is doing bad, why are we accepting it and not saying anything? If we say nothing, we are just as much in the wrong. We've just got to do better as people.

ENVISIONING WHAT IS POSSIBLE

THIS JOURNEY IN a very large sense is about agency. About how we shape it, how we tap into it, how we sustain it. Still more specifically, it's about how we marry empowerment to our love for the world, what matters to us, what wrongs we want to right, and what collective dreams we hope to realize. Whether that's resolving conflicts with a crotchety neighbor or combating global warming, certain fundamental principles and practices of mindfulness can lead to the clarity and confidence that let us take that next step.

This is a journey about envisioning what is possible. I remember going to see an old farmhouse for sale down the road from the Insight Meditation Society in Barre, Massachusetts, which I co-founded in 1976 with Joseph Goldstein and Jack Kornfield. I went with Joseph and a friend, Sarah Doering. The farmhouse, as far as I could tell, was simply falling apart. Joseph and Sarah chatted happily. "Well, we could try to move this wall, or at least open up that passageway . . . Underneath this wrecked floor might well lie hidden beauty . . . What if we built a small addition onto that door for a porch?"

Finally I broke in with, "Please, let's not buy it." I just couldn't imagine it looking like anything much different from what it looked like right then, even if repainted or tidied up. In my mind, it was forever dilapidated, forlorn, and in disrepair.

They didn't listen to me at all. I realized the vision of what was possible had already been formed in each of their minds. Their visions may not have been identical, but each was bold and, importantly, realizable. They weren't overly idealistic visions bound to be doomed by impossible fund-raising shortfalls or the prospect of too much work—except in *my mind*. I realized they were actually holding the vision of *what it was* and the vision of *what it could be* simultaneously. Change would take resources—time, effort, community, money—but the spark that would get things started was to believe that the vision was possible in the first place.

I'm not skilled at seeing the seeds of longed-for transformation in a building. I'm better at seeing it in people. I've looked many times at a friend in the throes of a terrible divorce or other devastating loss and been able to picture their healing and expansive happiness. I can see it in front of me, like a faint but discernible silhouette amid the chaos and pain of their current situation. And I've been right.

And when I am in touch with the perspective and sense of openness that my meditation practice has strengthened in me, I very much see the healing we are capable of—in communities, in cultures, in this world.

Over many decades, bell hooks has highlighted the ways our systems can oppress. She has found much to be enraged about, and yet her consistent message is about love. As she told me recently, "I've always said that love is a practice, and like most things we practice, it is difficult. That truth contrasts with everyone thinking love is easy, but what about when we encounter people we don't want to love? There are times I get up in the morning, and I think, *Okay. Who am I to love today?* That is not a choice based on who I think is cute or who I want to spend time with, but it's the recognition of the hunger we all have for love."

Like bell, I believe that the love we crave, and that we have available to give, is a healing force. Love is not soft and mushy. It is strong and resilient. It springs from the truth of our interconnectedness and is powerful because it is aligned with what is true.

I believe in the possibility of a world where our interconnection is a deeply known and motivating force, where no one is left out, where the innate dignity of every person is acknowledged, and where hatred and fear and greed can be tempered. I believe in a world where change might be hard but is *always* seen as possible, however stuck we might feel in any given moment. I believe in a world where we can have wisdom to guide us, we can have love to propel us, and we can have the support of one another to try to accomplish a vision of inclusion and care. I also believe in justice, in a world where actions have consequences, where people are held accountable even as we try to take care of one another.

And I believe in a world where the fluidity and softness of love—like water—might superficially seem like the weakest thing of all, but lo and behold, it is indomitable. It can even wear away rock.

What kind of world do you most deeply believe in?

PRACTICE: GATHERING OUR ENERGY

THIS CLASSIC MEDITATION practice is designed to strengthen the force of concentration. If you consider how scattered, how distracted, how out of the moment we may ordinarily be, you can see the benefit of gathering our attention and our energy. All of that energy could be available to us but usually isn't because we throw it away into distraction. We can gather all of that attention and energy to become integrated, to have a center, to not be so fragmented and torn apart, to be empowered.

In this system, the breath we focus on is the normal flow of the in and out breath. We don't try to make the breath deeper or different, we simply encounter it however it's appearing and however it's changing.

To begin with, you can sit comfortably and relax. You don't have to feel self-conscious, as though you are about to do something special or weird. Just be at ease. It helps if your back can be straight, without being strained or overarched. You can close your eyes or not, however you feel comfortable.

Notice where the feeling of the breath is most predominant—at the nostrils, at the chest, or at the abdomen. Rest your attention lightly, in just that area. See if you can feel just one breath, from the beginning, through the middle, to the end. If you're with the breath at the nostrils, it may be tingling, vibration, warmth, coolness. If at the abdomen, it may be movement, pressure, stretching, release. You don't have to name these sensations, but feel them. It's just one breath.

And if images or sounds, emotions, sensations arise, but they're not strong enough to actually take you away from the feeling of the breath, just let them flow on by. You don't have to follow after them, you don't have to attack them; you're breathing. It's like seeing a friend in a crowd; you don't have to shove everyone else aside or make them go away, but your enthusiasm, your interest, is going toward your friend—"Oh, there's my friend. There's the breath."

When something arises—sensations, emotions, thoughts, whatever it might be—that's strong enough to take your attention away from the feeling of the breath, or if you've fallen asleep, or if you get lost in some incredible fantasy, see if you can let go of the distraction and begin again, bringing your attention back to the breath. If you have to let go and begin again thousands of times, it's fine; that's the practice.

You may notice the rhythm of your breath changing in the course of this meditation session. You can just allow it to be however it is. Whatever arises, you can shepherd your attention back to the feeling of the breath.

Remember that in letting go of distraction, the important word is *gentle*. We can gently let go, we can forgive ourselves for having wandered and with great kindness to ourselves, we can begin again.

When you feel ready, you can open your eyes. See if you can bring this awareness of breath periodically into your day.

2

AGENCY

✳

THE STATUE OF LIBERTY HAS long been an object of rever-
ence for me. I am fascinated by her compassion, transported
by her dignity and strength. I've publicly confessed to owning any
number of blue-green objects meant to be her, each made of glass,
or crystal, or whatever erasers are made of. I once joked about
wanting to buy a five-foot replica to put in the small New York
City studio apartment I was subletting—to bring this emblem of

welcoming into my home. Mostly, I was joking about it. Mostly. I am a genuine fangirl.

The grace of the Statue of Liberty is perfectly expressed by the inscription by Emma Lazarus at its base. Naming Lady Liberty "the Mother of Exiles," Lazarus writes in her voice:

Give me your tired, your poor,
Your huddled masses yearning to breathe free,
The wretched refuse of your teeming shore.
Send these, the homeless, tempest-tost to me,
I lift my lamp beside the golden door!

Millions of people, immigrants (like my grandparents) and visitors, have come upon those words, a lightning bolt declaring, "Here's a chance." She's someone saying, "Welcome. You have a home here. You, too, belong here." She lifts the light of arrival. That iconic welcome is her best-known action.

The Statue of Liberty welcomes us all home to ourselves, that intrinsic part of us that—no matter what—deserves love, happiness, respect, and a place to rest. This is our universal goal, the inchoate yearning held in our common humanity, what we're all striving for in ourselves . . . and if we're able, for one another.

That sense of striving begins with agency—taking a concept that can be abstract or distant and breathing life into it, daring to imagine that dreams can come true, and determining to try. Anyone who has ever lost a job and doesn't know who they are anymore; or who has been rejected by the love of their life and needs to start anew not quite knowing what's real or who can be trusted; or who has woken up at night wondering if they're worth anything at all; or who has felt defined by physical illness, intense emotional distress, stifling circumstances of poverty or trauma or disenfranchisement by others—any of us who have had these experiences has a sense of the significant wherewithal it takes to stir up a push toward action.

In the previous chapter, we looked at daring to imagine a future that looks different from the past or the present. Here, we consider what it takes to make that real.

If you look carefully at the Statue of Liberty, you see that the back of her right foot is raised. She is in midstride. As Dave Eggers said in his book about the statue, *Her Right Foot,* "This 150-foot woman is on the go." Lady Liberty is ready to spring into action. She is moving forward to help quell fear, to embrace lonely strangers, to pick up the discarded and bring them all the way home. Her step represents action, activity, aliveness. It isn't just the sense of movement I find inspiring. It's also the sense of purpose animating the movement, reminding all of their inherent worth, that they belong.

WAKE-UP CALLS

SOMETIMES IT IS an intense and personal experience that not only wakes us up but impels us to act to try to make a difference. It isn't always this way, of course. Pain and loss and challenge can easily cause us to turn completely inward, enveloped by our situation. On every level—cellular, physical, emotional—we are curled into the fetal position, trying to absorb the shock of sudden change. It's like having an infection, where the defenses of the body rush to the affected site to wall it off. Our sensitivity, our awareness, our compassion can so easily be blocked, especially when we're trying to bear a great magnitude of pain. Perhaps, being human, we are inevitably blocked for a while. But for some, the story doesn't end there. It progresses, leading to an inclusive and expansive caring for others. The fight/flight/freeze reaction, blunt and automatic, refines into a response that is active and engaged. We want things to be better for others. We look for meaning, connection, a purpose to our day.

CHOOSING TO CARE AND CHOOSING TO ACT

IN THE PAST decade, attorney Ady Barkan has helped improve the lives of millions of people: he co-authored the law that guarantees paid sick days to all workers in New York City; he helped end the abuse of stop-and-frisk practices that unfairly targeted black and Latinx New Yorkers; and he moved the Federal Reserve to adopt policies that prioritize job creation and wage growth for the American public.

Then, in October 2016, when he was thirty-two years old and his son was only four months, he was diagnosed with amyotrophic lateral sclerosis (ALS), often referred to as Lou Gehrig's disease (after the baseball player who was diagnosed with it in 1939). Not long after Barkan was diagnosed with an illness that progressively breaks down all the muscles in the body, he went from being able to run on a California beach to relying on a wheelchair and facing mortality.

The diagnosis left Barkan with a profound choice about whether to retreat or continue on the path that had formed the basis of his life. He decided he would keep trying to make a difference to others, as long as that was possible. And he has done so without the bitterness and self-pitying that's so tempting to drift into when we are faced with the worst.

Talking about his attitude in an email message, which he reproduced in his book *Eyes to the Wind*, he said:

The truth is I've had an amazing hand so far in life. Compared to the billions in abject poverty, the tens of millions killed in war, the untold number who aren't happy, I've been very lucky. So rather than bemoan "Why me?"—which I certainly have the urge to do almost every moment—I want to be happy and energized and squeeze every last drop out of what I've got left.

So, I am now moving full steam ahead trying to seize these last few months/years and live them to the fullest—including being with Rachel and Carl and friends and family, doing some beautiful things.

Barkan described his and his wife's practice as focusing on what they had left, not on what they had lost; remembering to breathe; and staying active and involved in the moment. He has focused his efforts on turning out voters to elect candidates who will protect health care programs for Americans. Ironically, his very disease makes him a potent spokesperson for maintaining and extending affordable health care.

A SENSE OF PURPOSE

SAMANTHA NOVICK ALSO woke up one day to an event that radically changed her life and her view of the future. Samantha graduated from Marjory Stoneman Douglas High School in 2008. Her mother, Sharon Cutler, is a teacher there and was at school on February 14, 2018, when, as we noted in chapter 1, a gunman killed seventeen students and staff and wounded seventeen others. Her father, Ken Cutler, is a local politician who sits on the Parkland City Commission. The tragedy mobilized Samantha to take action and help to organize a historic march against gun violence that attracted national attention.

When I asked Samantha about what motivated her to action, rather than freezing, in the aftermath of an event more horrible than she could have imagined, she said:

It's like we were suddenly and unexpectedly hit by a huge meteor that left a giant crater in the middle of our lives, our community. And some were hit directly, like those students who were in the building or saw things no person, let alone a young person, should ever have to see. People lost friends, spouses, children.

This giant thing descended, hit us out of nowhere, and left this huge hole. For those who weren't directly hit, it was a bit easier for us in the beginning. A bunch of us just grabbed shovels, if you will, and did whatever we could to try to fill up the hole, but as time goes on, we see that the hole is never going to be filled. It's just not. But if there is anything I can do to help one person or to further the cause of non-violence in any way, it would be irresponsible not to act.

I don't think I'm being entirely altruistic. Because it's also been helpful for me. There seems to be a sort of a self-serving purpose behind throwing yourself into activism, because it helps you heal. It feels good to not just sit there and stare at the hole. It feels good to do something, to start filling it in, no matter how impossibly deep it is.

As these potent examples of action in the midst of personal and societal tragedy demonstrate, agency is that purposeful, embodied, heartfelt movement from deep within, and we know it when we're experiencing it. A fire is stoked inside us, and while hopelessness and despair may arise, they also recede as a sense of purpose steadies us and moves us forward. We have control over so little—a truth that is sometimes exceptionally bitter—but we can choose to care, and we can choose to act. That is the truth that frees us.

It's also possible that intense, personal pain might not be the thing that causes us to take that step forward. Maybe we see the effects of discrimination on the cousin we grew up with who recently came out as gay. Or we hear our friend's biracial child was refused the use of a bathroom by a clerk in a small store. Or a colleague is overcome by addiction to pain medication, and we see both that they are not evil and that there are very few available or affordable services that can help them. Or we take the time to talk to someone very different from ourselves, and when we discover how much we are essentially the same, their lives and concerns become palpable, real.

I was recently hospitalized with a severe infection, which brought me into close contact with a series of professional caregivers. I've long been an admirer of Ai-jen Poo, director of the National Domestic Workers Alliance, co-director of Caring Across Generations, working to ensure better treatment and basic rights for these very hardworking people. I've offered some meditation classes and met quite lovely people in Ai-jen's organization. I've been at the margins of the movement to ensure rights for domestic workers. I've been to many funerals of the mother or father of a friend, where "Gladys" or "Marjorie" or "Sonia" is profusely thanked, some caregiver the rest of us didn't know. The comment is usually "She saved us" or "She enabled my mother or father to die at home, with dignity."

In the months I spent recuperating, thanks to a friend's great generosity, I had twenty-four-hour home health aides as other friends kindly opened their home to me. Given my limitations in strength and mobility at the time, having the aides saved me from needing to be in a skilled nursing home as I got better.

Throughout that period, I was basically spending my time with a set of new roommates. So of course, we talked. I learned that one person had another job earlier in the day and could only work a later shift. One used her only days off to take her father to dialysis. There were stories of child support never materializing; of coming into this kind of work having taken care of a dying parent; of moving up in the world from picking raspberries and appreciating the good feeling that you are making a difference in someone's life. Because of the way our culture at large views the work of home health aides, if you have not used their services the people who do it are often somewhat invisible, as is their humanity, their struggle. They are invisible in part because their work makes us think of infirmity, death, isolation, losing capacities, and shame at not being perfect and in control.

Now they were very real to me. Any abstraction I had felt earlier, even as I had admired Ai-jen and tried to contribute to her work through my work, fell away. I now feel committed to not forgetting them or allowing them to "disappear" again.

Agency takes over when it isn't enough to simply feel bad about a situation, write a disconsolate tweet, or vaguely note that something should be done. It's like the ignition being turned on. We care for ourselves and others and don't stop at caring. Now we breathe vitality into that caring. Our values cease to exist only as abstractions, and we cease being a mere bystander to life.

THIS SENSE OF agency to remake our own lives or the world that we see can happen at any time, at any age. As Dorothy Allison, author of *Bastard out of Carolina,* said, "If I could have found what I needed at thirteen, I would not have lost so much of my life chasing vindication or death. Give some child, some thirteen-year-old, the hope of the remade life."

Mindfulness teacher and community organizer Shelly Tygielski is an example of someone getting switched on at a young age. She grew up in an enormously insular Orthodox Jewish family in Israel. Her first experience with activism came after she moved to the United States with her family when she was twelve years old and made friends with a girl named Jennifer. "She had the most beautiful red hair," Shelly remembers, "and she came from a conservative Jewish family. Which was a curious thing for me. I had never met a Conservative or Reform Jew."

Jennifer came to Shelly's house for the Sabbath, and at dinner, when Shelly's mother served the main course, Jennifer politely refused. "I'm a vegetarian," she explained. Shelly's mind was blown. "I was like, 'Wait, what? That's a thing? Hold on a second.'" Shelly had never liked eating meat, but in her household, you ate whatever was on the dinner table. For her, this was a pivotal moment. "So it was then that I thought, *That's it. I'm a vegetarian.*"

Jennifer continued to expand Shelly's concepts of how kids can take a stand and make a difference. It was the mid-'80s and Jennifer was aware of and concerned about the social issues making headlines at the time. "When I would go to her house," Shelly recalls, "one of our playdate activities was to canvass the neighborhood—door-to-door. We'd get signatures to save the whales or to boycott companies that tested products on animals. She was really involved in Greenpeace and PETA."

Shelly had never felt such power before, such a capacity to make a difference. "We even got our school policy to change, making them start their first recycling program." The lesson soaked in deep. "It was really exciting to see that when you believe in something, you can organize people and convince them to change for the positive."

Those first experiences with activism, Shelly says, changed everything, and her life since then has revolved around making a difference in the world. As a mindfulness teacher, she has continually offered classes to the Parkland community in the wake of the shooting at Marjory Stoneman Douglas High School. In 2019, Shelly and I co-created a retreat for survivors of gun violence—people who had lost children, people who had been shot themselves, people who had tried desperately to protect others at the scene of a tragedy.

We bring alive a vision by taking that crucial first step toward making it real—sometimes out of inspiration, sometimes out of outrage, sometimes faltering, and sometimes with resolve. To step forward toward a life of caring and engagement, we challenge our conditioning: the fear, the believing of ourselves or others unworthy, the incorporating of limiting stories we have been told about ourselves and about life. We take on what is holding us back—and there is a lot that can hold us back—starting with feeling we are not worthy.

WHEN SELF-WORTH TAKES A BEATING

SO MANY OF us feel ourselves to be lesser, left out, and perhaps not worthy of even our own respect. I can't recount how many people I have met in my years of teaching meditation who have been inflicted with such low self-esteem, who have been so hurt and downtrodden, that they've felt utterly immobilized.

When you feel that low, it may be necessary to seek help, to find your tribe, to seek out those who will make it their mission to lift you up. So often these are people who have been lifted up themselves and want to pass that on to others.

I'm reminded of seeing Viola Davis accept the Golden Globe Award for her supporting actress role in the film adaptation of August Wilson's classic *Fences*. The award recognized her poignant portrayal of the neglected and abused housewife Rose Lee Maxson in the movie, and in her speech, Davis spoke directly to those who have experienced sexual abuse or assault and tend to think of themselves as worthless and to blame: "There's no prerequisites to worthiness," she said. "You're born worthy, and I think that's a message a lot of women need to hear. The women who are still in silence because of trauma, shame, due to the assault—they need to understand that it's not their fault and they're not dirty."

Respecting ourselves may not appear to be a radical act—but it is. It is both radical and impactful. When we care, and when we know we are worthy, we can be agents of change—for ourselves and for others.

Shantel Walker, the fast-food worker we met in chapter 1, was able to organize workers and press for fair wages because she knew that she, and they, were worth something: "I took action because my family had always let me know I was worthy, and I knew therefore I was worth more than how I was being treated. I knew others were worth more and maybe didn't know it. I had to stand up for myself and for them."

TO CELEBRATE JOSEPH Goldstein's sixtieth birthday, some of our close friends rented a boat to sail around New York Harbor. It was a really fun experience, with chanting, a great Indian meal, and loving friends and family—amusingly, there was even the surprise appearance of teenage Joseph's bar mitzvah portrait.

Despite my otherwise happy feelings, and my wearing a magical acupuncture wristband meant to prevent seasickness, I started to feel ill. I'd experienced a lot of motion sickness as a child, but not much really since, even while following a lifestyle of perpetual travel. Seasickness is a ghastly feeling, one that I tried to smile over on the boat so as not to spoil the mood. But looking back, I suspect my smile was more grimace-like than anything and, as the party went on, began to increasingly convey, "Just put me out of my misery."

And then the boat drew close to the Statue of Liberty.

There she stood, 305 feet high from the base and pedestal to the tip of her torch, broken chains at her feet, welcoming those who have often been through a long and harrowing journey. I was enraptured. If little eraser replicas make me happy, imagine what the real thing does! My queasiness and unease disappeared. Only then did I remember that as a child, I'd only begun getting motion sickness once I had turned nine. I had lived with my parents until I was four and they divorced. Then I lived with my mother until I was nine and she died, which was when I moved in with my paternal grandparents.

In that period of my life, any mode of transportation—buses, cars, trains—would leave me heaving. And I remembered just as suddenly that as a child, I would only get sick leaving home—I never had any trouble at all, on any kind of vehicle, on the way back. I was just so generally afraid, so unanchored, that having any less of a ground overwhelmed me.

Sometimes it is scary to leave home, which is why it brings such a profound feeling of relief to realize we can carry a sense of home within—of knowing who we are—energizing and enlivening, as we step forward, stepping over or into and beyond our fear.

COUNTING ON OTHERS AND SEEKING SALVATION FROM OUTSIDE OURSELVES

I THINK OF the Statue of Liberty in contrast to other iconic women, women who wait. I think of the architectural feature known as a *captain's walk,* or less auspiciously, a *widow's walk,* seen in some nineteenth-century North American coastal homes. The latter name, folklore has it, refers to the wives of seamen standing there, waiting, pacing, looking out to a sea that had very likely taken their husbands out of their homes and into hers. Women pacing in fear, waiting to be completed by something or someone external, waiting to receive rather than to give, waiting to come alive. And waiting some more.

When I was living with my father's parents, I was the quintessential person just waiting. And waiting. No missing husband, but a strong sense of a missing life. I was going through the days as though I were a tape recorder with the Pause button on. My entire life, up until I was eighteen, I'd felt on the margins, different, left out. I'd felt numb, or couldn't think what to do, or I was convinced my doing anything was a futile gesture. I was helpless to move, to effect change. Suddenly, I wanted a chance for things to be truly different.

Early on, I made a key decision that determined the entire

course of my adult life: applying to the American Studies department at the university I attended. In it, I asked to spend my junior year in India studying meditation. I think of that moment so often. I was seventeen when I applied, eighteen when I left. I had grown up in New York City and had not even been to California when I sent in that application. How was I not content to simply be a scholar, studying comparative religion maybe? Because of that essential and mysterious and impactful moment, when I'm asked now what my major was in college, I often joke, "Alchemy." It was kind of like that.

On my journey, I took a longing as ephemeral as skywriting and embodied it. I didn't think I'd be nauseated the whole long trip to the other end of the world (and I wasn't), but I suspected I'd be frightened for a lot of it (which I was). I went anyway.

I was hoping to find relief from my own personal suffering, but that journey formed the foundation for my lifetime of work and service in this world. Anything I intuited about listening within, or working through suffering, or caring about myself to care for others was reinforced and intensified and elevated by the practices of mindfulness and lovingkindness that I later discovered.

We can all move off the margins of our lives, the feeling of just watching and waiting for . . . something. We can discover which limitations are crafted by cynicism or hopelessness, and go past them into the center of change, giving life to what we care about.

BELIEVING THE STORIES OTHERS
TELL ABOUT US

ONE AFTERNOON, I was presenting a workshop with bell hooks at the bell hooks Institute in Berea, Kentucky. At one point, I spoke about how others might tell a story about us—about our worthiness and whether we belong or not, whether we're included—and we take it in. That story might permeate our being until it becomes *our* story. We reshape our identity around it. Someone in the room said, "I don't get that. People don't tell stories about us. They don't necessarily know us."

I meant what I was saying to include not only narratives that people might say about us specifically but also the stories that a group of people or an institution might impose on us, even in very subtle ways, such as through architecture. The Insight Meditation Society, in Barre, Massachusetts, which I mentioned in the first chapter, has a stunning colonnade in front, four columns, two stories high, with seven stairs leading up to a large front door.

It turns out what I had always thought of as grand and inspiring told another story to another class of people: wheelchair users. It became clear that we needed to build a new ramp. It can be very difficult to retrofit an old building, and building a ramp in front was going to result in something that would be huge, not necessarily in harmony with the original architecture, and restrict the driveway. That's why we had put the ramp in the back in the first place.

In the end, we decided the ramp must go out front, because of the story that it tells: you are part of what happens here, you are welcome, along with everyone else; please come through the front door. It may be troublesome—I, for one, am not great at navigating the driveway in my car—but it tells a story about who belongs, and that counts for everything.

At that same workshop in Kentucky, bell hooks offered another example of a behavior, a way of acting in the world, that told a very potent story of who is of worth and who isn't. Growing up, bell would frequently see a rich white gentleman who dressed up his dog in a fancy outfit and sat the dog in the front seat of his car, while he kept his black maid riding in the back seat. *How could someone do that?* she thought, as it seemed to her that he honored a dog more than a person.

That left an indelible impression in young bell's mind. It has taken her a lot of work on love over the years to counteract the kinds of stories she has experienced people telling about her place in the world based on her skin color.

Merck CEO Ken Frazier told *The New York Times* a story from the days of apartheid about seeing how deep-seated stories could ingrain behavior:

> I lived one whole semester in Soweto. It was completely lawless. There were no streetlights. It was a completely separated area where people were contained, because the South African government's job, as it saw it, was to separate blacks from whites.
>
> But what I remember more than anything else was interacting with people who their entire lives had been told that they were second class, that they were inferior, and how hard it was to get people, particularly the men, to speak up in audible tones, because they had been in many ways told that their voice was not worth listening to. In addition to trying to teach people the substantive legal issues, it was a lot about trying to instill self-confidence.

BIG FORCES BEYOND OUR CONTROL

WHAT PREVENTS US from taking action may have to do with getting caught up in forces beyond our control, as opposed to being beaten down by the specific circumstances of our individual lives, or being defined by the stories others make up about us. Think about poverty, or institutionalization, or disenfranchisement—all of which rigorously patrol the boundaries of what we even think we're allowed to imagine for ourselves. When I consider these large, powerful forces, they bring up the feeling of collapse, when we grow numb, when we opt to stop caring because hope really does seem like the cruelest thing.

When I visited former countries of the Soviet Union after its breakup, I was struck by how little sense of agency people seemed to have. In this state of chaos, they were unsure of how to behave. They had been paralyzed by being conditioned not to act, taught to be passive observers of their own lives. I was taken by the fact that they took refuge in incessant sarcasm and cynicism. It gave them, I think, a false sense of agency, a way to feel that they were responding to their conditions, taking some kind of action, when in fact they were mired in inaction, because they couldn't see any way *to* act.

Being tied to a system that drains our agency conditions us to futility and defeat. I think of a friend who told me a story about being seven or eight years old, living with her divorced mother and her maternal uncle. The details are dim, she says, but she remembers her uncle breaking her mother's arm and then a social worker coming (they were living on public assistance). The social worker refused to supplement the mother's rent so that the mother could move out, saying my friend had already lost her father and would be harmed by losing her uncle, too.

I don't know specifically what impact this had on the mother, but my friend recalls she wasn't asked about *her* preferences. Since she was a child, it was assumed her voice didn't count.

Something just gave up inside her then, and she has worked her entire adult life to mold a sense of agency and to protect and preserve it, having known what it means to live in a mental state of powerlessness.

I was walking with another friend through the streets of New York one evening after dinner when we were approached for money by a man who had clearly been living on the streets. My friend was newly sober and was concerned the man might use the money to buy some booze. She said, "I won't give you money, but let's go into this deli and you can choose whatever you want to eat. I'll pay for it." The three of us entered, and I watched the man go through stages of disbelief, intimidation, dawning acceptance, and finally delight. He kept checking, "Really anything I want?"

"Anything?"

"I can choose extra cheese?"

I was once again struck by the toxic humiliation and powerlessness society often pairs with poverty, binding them together and sealing them tight: "If you can't afford much, you're pretty worthless. You don't look tight, nicely prosperous, or predictable."

I thought a lot about choice, about belonging, about having a vision and dreams and a reasonable path to at least try to achieve them.

The man in the deli could not have looked more elated. Having so little choice in his life, he seemed to savor the novelty of being treated with respect, as an individual with his own needs and desires. I learned a lot watching this powerful exchange: a moment of paying attention to someone can often switch on a glimmer of self-worth in another who seems completely bereft.

WE ALL HAVE SOMETHING TO GIVE

I DERIVE THE same inspiration from two stories of one place, told from different angles. It offers us the recognition that *everyone* has something to give, that no one is excluded from the possibility of agency. In 1999, Killian Noe moved to Seattle and teamed up with a group of people to found Recovery Café. The group was committed to tackling a challenge that keeps so many people homeless and unable to lift themselves up: addiction. Recovery Café is a community of people who have—as their About Us statement says—"been traumatized by homelessness, addiction, and other mental health challenges." Their mission, they go on to say, is to "[come] to know ourselves as loved with gifts to share." It's a place people can come to when they're sober to find, and offer, community and companionship to others, and it has grown from a small storefront to a facility that takes up an entire triangular city block and houses a School for Recovery. Today there are eighteen Recovery Cafés in ten states and the District of Columbia. The next one is slated to open in Vancouver, British Columbia, in 2020.

"To know ourselves as loved," as their statement says, speaks to the heart of the matter. Killian herself says that the café serves personal needs that she has, as well: "I, too, need community to reflect back my self-worth." When she talked to us about the guiding principles of the café, she provided a wonderful definition of what agency means, particularly in terms of elevated self-worth:

> We intentionally call the people we serve here *members*, not *clients*, because we want them to know that this is a place of belonging. This is not just a social service agency where you go to receive services. It's a place where you come and

you contribute to the community. You take ownership for the community. You help the community thrive not only by contributing to helping to run the café—one of the commitments is that everyone must pitch into the actual work—but also by showing up for each other. That's the biggest contribution: giving yourself.

Jenna Crow is a member of Recovery Café. A service veteran, Jenna was sexually assaulted in the army and came back to the United States with PTSD after her discharge. Through a series of complications, she had trouble getting benefits and ended up homeless in Seattle for a year.

Like so many people, Jenna felt a lack of self-respect, and she silenced herself (which is something we do when we feel unwanted and unloved). She felt powerless. She made her way finally to Recovery Café, which was a key part of her rediscovery of purpose and power. A turning point came one night at a café open mic night. Jenna played flute directly to a man who came in highly agitated. She saw that it soothed him. "I understood what his reality is like," Jenna said, "because I've been in that reality. It was a moment of focus, where I was a person who was able to alleviate his suffering. I'm getting goose bumps right now thinking about it. You suddenly have this moment of clarity and you understand, 'I am poised to do something that is going to alleviate this person's suffering.'"

When Jenna saw that she gets to give back, she discovered her worth, her agency, in doing something for others, no matter how small, or unexpected and spontaneous, the gesture.

Jenna is thankful for what the staff have done to help in her recovery, through their "ministry of presence," essentially being there with her and for her through thick and thin. "They held the space for me is another way of putting it. And eventually, I was on the recovery road. I came out of my little shell." Jenna became a facilitator at Recovery Café and went on to take recovery coach training and continues to increase her contribution to the community through mentoring others and being mentored *by* others.

WHERE TO PUT OUR ENERGY?

HOW DO WE know where to focus *our* action? After all, there's a lot of pain in this world. Part of the answer lies in discerning under what circumstances we *will* take a step forward. Playwright Lin-Manuel Miranda has said, "You cannot let all the world's tragedies into your heart. You'll drown. But the ones you do let in should count. Let them manifest action."

Similarly, historian Howard Zinn, author of the classic *A People's History of the United States*, offered this advice: "I would encourage people to look around them in their community and find an organization that is doing something that they believe in, even if that organization has only five people, or ten people, or twenty people, or a hundred people. . . . When enough people do enough things, however small they are, then change takes place."

Once we summon the energy to declare, "This is what I believe in as true and just," then we can go for it.

And we keep exploring the nature of the energy that moves change—what nourishes it, what dampens it, what untangles it, what distorts it—as we look toward sustaining caring and engagement during our life's journey.

PRACTICE: EXPLORING OUR STORY LINES

WE DO THIS practice to develop a different relationship to the stories others tell about us and the stories we tell ourselves about who we are and what we are capable of. Please sit comfortably, with either your eyes closed or slightly open, however you feel most at ease.

You can begin by bringing your attention to the breath, wherever you feel it most predominantly—the nostrils, chest, or abdomen. You can rest your attention on whatever sensations you find there as you breathe naturally. The breath is like our home base—if during the course of this session you feel lost or like too much is going on, you can just return your attention to the feeling of the breath.

See what thoughts may be present in your awareness. Allow yourself to notice thoughts arising as events in the mind. Experience thoughts coming and going in each moment without pushing them away or being carried off by them. Perhaps experience thoughts like clouds passing through the open sky of your awareness. Some heavy and thunderous, some light and airy, being aware of them all, exploring with gentle interest and curiosity.

It may be helpful to experience thoughts as boats passing along a river. Some passing so silently that you barely notice, some so unpleasant that your attention turns away, others so compelling that they highjack your attention and carry you far down the river. Explore the thoughts arising in your mind, noticing when you are pushing them away or being highjacked by them, and coming back again and again to noticing, taking a seat by the river, observing thoughts passing by.

As a habit, certain thought patterns arise that we tend to get lost in, overcome by, defined by, even as we resent or fear them. We can retrain our whole mental attitude by first learning to recognize these patterns and perhaps even calmly naming them: "Oh, here is the pattern of thinking, *Everything is wrong,* the pattern of thinking, *I'm a failure,* the pattern of thinking, *I can never do enough.*"

Once we recognize them, we can remind ourselves that they are just visiting. They are not essentially who we are. We couldn't stop them from visiting, but we can let them go. Even if they return a thousand times a session, they still have the same nature— they are visiting, we don't have to invite them to move in, we don't have to blame ourselves for their coming, and we can learn to let them go.

After you finish this formal session of practice, you can explore bringing this skill of gentle interest, curiosity, and attention to your thoughts into your encounters throughout the day.

3

AWAKENING TO THE FIRE

✳

When Anger Turns to Courage

F OR MOST PEOPLE, SIMPLY GETTING through an ordinary day comes with challenges. We manage routine obligations, filter new input, navigate emotions we're only partially connected to, and absorb the rituals of casual encounters. We power through, but on autopilot—our energy is sapped, our reserves are tapped out. We are somewhat asleep, half-conscious, distracted.

What jolts us awake?

Sometimes it's an encounter with the unexpected, such as an

abrupt change or the shock of suffering, whether that's our own suffering or that of others. There is violence in our hometown. A devastating hurricane destroys a city. A friend struggles with addiction, and his family can't afford treatment. A cousin reveals a recent experience of domestic violence, and yet her ex is able to procure a gun. Those shocks snap us out of our hermetic dream state, prompting us to look more deeply within ourselves and at the world around us. It may take something compelling to wake us up, to turn us away from that half-asleep state and away from the easy answers society offers us about how best to live: consume more, compete more, move faster, get ahead of change.

When we are shaken awake by events, the energy that's often released first is anger. In activist circles, there's an old adage that declares, "If you're not outraged, you're not paying attention." As free speech activist and writer Soraya Chemaly has said, "Anger . . . is actually a signal emotion: It warns us of indignity, threat, insult, and harm." When an interaction, person, or experience makes us angry, our bodies and minds are effectively having an emotional "immune" response. We are telling ourselves to self-protect, the same way blood rushes to the site of an insect bite. It is often anger that turns our heart-thudding distress into action, that pushes us to actively protect someone's right to be happy, to be healthy, to be whole.

If somebody violates our bodies or our space or our work, pushing past a point of acceptable infringement, anger is what re-establishes our boundaries, clarifies our integrity, and insists, "Get back." If we ourselves are humiliated, it's often anger that has us stand up and say, "That's not who I am." If another's words or actions are attempting to define us, it's often anger that demands we reclaim our own narratives, that we pay attention. If we are trivialized, or lied to, or overlooked, anger asserts, "I am worth more than that!"

The late farmworker activist Cesar Chavez believed that moral outrage could produce change, according to Marshall Ganz, who worked with Chavez as a labor organizer for sixteen years. "You can't organize a group of victims," Ganz said in an interview for *The Atlantic* magazine. "If people only see themselves that way, there's no sense of agency, no sense of power. But when you tell them that we're fighting an injustice or an offense to their dignity, they become angry and involved."

When we see that someone is being excluded, threatened, or victimized, anger gives us a voice. "They are worth more than that!" we shout. I am still in touch with my friend who was the little girl in the previous chapter, the one whose mother's arm was broken by her own brother, who was living with them. Now all grown up, she's still angry that her mother was not supported in her effort to change households, and she channels that into her advocacy for children. When she was a child herself, no one asked if she was afraid, if she could sleep, if she felt okay being left alone with her uncle. Her anger is her assertion of self-worth: "I am someone worth listening to. Even way back then, I should have had a voice."

Anger helps us buck social niceties and point out problems, sometimes leaving us the only ones willing to do so—everyone else in the room may be pointedly looking the other way. That tendency to see and name what's wrong also contains an aspect of the introspective experience that shows up in many meditation practices: moving past the superficial level of perception, being ready to look deeper than others are inclined to and being willing to honestly recognize what is unpleasant or unwelcome. It's commonly the angry person in a group, for example, who points out the flaw or mistake or problem that everyone else is studiously avoiding.

The energy of anger can be useful, but how hard it can be to contain! I first met Mallika Dutt when we sat on a conference panel together. She is the founder of Inter-Connected, an initiative that uplifts the interdependent nature of self, community, and planet to advance collective well-being. Mallika was born in India but has lived in the United States for many years. She has dedicated her life to creating a world where love and compassion rule, but at the same time, she's based much of her work on outrage. It was outrage she felt more than twenty years ago while visiting a friend in an Indian hospital. The friend had had an accident, and the hospital's only available bed was in its burn unit. On her way in, Mallika passed other patients, women who had been doused in kerosene and set aflame by husbands and in-laws. "Bride burning" was a known practice in some regions of India, an unofficially sanctioned form of retaliation for unpaid dowries or suspected infidelities. Mallika's outrage at this rampant, often deadly, form of domestic violence and gender discrimination led her to found Breakthrough, an organization that uses popular culture media and community engagement to advance gender equality and social justice. Breakthrough has made a huge impact in India and beyond since its founding in 2000. Mallika has proved to be an amazing and tireless advocate for ending violence against women.

But even righteous anger can exact a cost.

After describing to our conference audience the violence she had borne witness to and the anger that arose as catapults to forging her life's work, Mallika said, "I don't know how to turn the anger off. I need to learn to dial it down. And not just me. It is manifest in my organization, in my relationships. I need to be able to develop a different relationship to it."

Mallika's comment reminded me that while the energy of anger might propel us to action, it also can be so entwined with fear or tunnel vision that it's ultimately destructive. There is a well-known quotation: "Anger is like swallowing poison hoping it kills the other guy." I thought Mahatma Gandhi had said it, but when I googled it, I saw it variously attributed to several others, including the Buddha, Nelson Mandela, Mark Twain, Carrie Fisher, Malachy McCourt, and Alcoholics Anonymous (AA). I guess it's just universal wisdom.

I do know it was the Buddha who said, "Anger, with its poisoned source and fevered climax, is murderously sweet." Most of us are familiar with the strangely addictive quality of anger—the rush of energy that pushes us to protest, to point out unpalatable truths, to draw a line. If we know that quality, we have likely also experienced how anger can become our default response, limiting our full range of perception. Anger can take over, as Mallika said. And it has the ability to cast away all self-doubt; after all, if we are on the side of righteousness, then how could we possibly fall into narrow or circumscribed thinking?

But we often do.

We may lash out from our anger or be paralyzed by it, and neither of those states is known for being a great source of problem-solving. When we dwell in a baseline feeling of anger, we tend to feel separate, alienated, and it's hard to think in constructive and open-minded ways. Look at any week's news—deaths far away, deaths close to home, cruelty, exploitation, inequality—how easy it is to move from outrage to anger to fixedness. I can certainly see that arc unfold in myself at times. One of the issues with chronic anger is the narrowed vision it fosters. Can we recognize the best way forward when we are so enraged?

In fact, in Buddhist psychology, anger is likened to a forest fire that burns up its own support. That means the anger can destroy the host, which is us. Dr. Barbara Fredrickson, a social psychologist and researcher based at the University of North Carolina at Chapel Hill, in a study of college student responses to crisis, found that "anger, fear, and anxiety . . . arouse people's autonomic nervous systems, producing increases in heart rate, vasoconstriction, and blood pressure, among other changes."

And like a forest fire, anger can burn wild, ending up in a place far from where it started and with devastating consequences. Who among us can look back at our lives—perhaps when we were relating to our children at times we felt under great stress; or when dealing with a parent unable or unwilling to face the reality of their aging; or after working hard at a project only to see it complicated or knocked down by the arrogance of a colleague—and not recall an instance of being so swept up by anger that we said or did something we now deeply regret?

Susan Davis has worked with various organizations within the international women's movement. Returning to the United States after doing productive work in Bangladesh, she was shocked to discover infighting between local organizations. "It was disillusioning," she said, especially to see that the leaders of those organizations were creating the culture of competition. "I think it was around scarcity mentality, around power and resources, those things. There could be different philosophies or ideologies at play. But there was basically a lot of unhealed stuff that would play out in room after room. For example, if people haven't dealt with their own sexual abuse and trauma, stuff they're working on, and they're trying to stop violence against women, it just spills out all over the room—the anger and the desire for revenge. And so all the blaming and shaming plays out."

Getting lost in anger can indeed leave us very far from where we want to be. That sarcastic comment we end an office discussion with soon becomes a point of offense among a broader sweep of our colleagues. An intemperate, scolding email undermines an alliance and threatens trust. For days on end we seem to notice only what's wrong, everywhere—the tiny burn mark on the carpet, the elevator music, the disgruntled expression on a commuter's face. Or we rigidly and rapidly categorize someone we disagree with and shift from seeing them as an adversary to seeing them as an enemy.

So often, the outcomes and behaviors born of being lost in anger are not pretty. Alcoholics Anonymous recognizes that *resentment*, anger's simmering cousin, is toxic to our inner lives. The case is plainly stated in the 12 Step group's core text, known as the *Big Book*, which first came out in 1939: "Resentment is the number one offender. It destroys more alcoholics than anything else." It's revealing to look at the word itself. *Resentment* is close to *re-sentiment*—*sentiment* meaning "feeling" and *re* meaning "again." So resentment is literally "feeling again." This gets to the heart of resentment: we cycle through old negative feelings or revisit old wrongs done to us by others. And do it again. And again.

It's as if each offending incident is captured on a video that loops in our minds. Resentment, in effect, is mentally replaying the scene countless times. As we do so, substantial wrongs grow overwhelming, and wrongs that are slight grow to huge proportions. This mental habit extracts tremendous costs. After all, resentment does nothing to change the person we resent. Nor does it resolve conflict. Instead of freeing us from the wrongs of others, resentment invites those people and incidents to dominate our thinking—a kind of emotional bondage.

And as friends of mine in AA have learned, if we are caught up in such cycles of resentment, what reserve of energy is left to focus on our own recovery?

SAVING THE FOREST

HOW DO WE move beyond the fire of anger and resentment? In Tibetan Buddhism, they say anger is what we reach for when we feel weak, because we think it will make us strong. So it functions to cover over a sense of helplessness, which for many of us is a nearly unbearable feeling. We want to *do*, we want to *fix*, we want *results* . . . we want *control*. The feeling of anger, in contrast to the disappointment and sorrow contained in helplessness, can convey, at least for a while, a sense of power, agency, pride, and righteousness.

Yet eventually, as James Baldwin said, "most people discover that when hate is gone, they will be forced to deal with their own pain." In an interview for the Harvard Divinity School's newsletter, Buddhist teacher Lama Rod Owens echoed Baldwin when he said, "Anger is always the bodyguard of our woundedness. There's the trauma, there's the anger, there's the rage, but healing is about moving through that. Not distancing, not distracting, but moving through it to that really fundamental sadness and hurt that's beneath the anger." Sooner or later, it becomes crucial to directly face that helplessness and pain: it is only when we can see them more as feelings born of circumstances in the moment than unassailable truths that we can start to genuinely move beyond them.

If we learn to not get so lost in anger but rather to mine its energy, we begin to act less out of a desperate need to assume control. We are able to act out of a determined, courageous marshaling of our resources to try to make a difference. As the Nobel Peace Prize laureate Kailash Satyarthi—a tireless advocate for the rights of enslaved children for over three decades—said in his 2015 TED talk, "If we are confined in the narrow shells of egos and the circles of selfishness, then the anger will turn out to be hatred, violence, revenge, destruction. But if we are able to break the circles, then the same anger could turn into a great power. We can break the circles by using our inherent compassion and connect with the world through compassion to make this world better."

In my lifetime, one of the most powerful shifts I've seen of moving from helplessness into courageous action has been in the evolution of the AIDS (acquired immunodeficiency syndrome) crisis in the United States. What first came to attention in the early 1980s as mysterious clusters of rare and devastating medical conditions prompted powerful grassroots community responses across the nation, which then prompted epidemiological discoveries and the birth of sustained and widespread activism. At first, though, people—primarily gay men and intravenous drug users—were getting sick and no one knew why. Fear of the unknown led to isolation and rejection of those who'd been infected with HIV (human immunodeficiency virus), and many of those suffering its outcomes were abandoned by family and by baffled medical workers. But there were also people who responded to this frightening, confusing epidemic with their humanity, who rerouted the course of their lives to care for loved ones, friends, and, sometimes, strangers.

I'm touched by the story of Ruth Coker Burks, an Arkansas woman who cared for hundreds of men as they died of AIDS in the 1980s. Back then, Burks was a twenty-five-year-old new mom and, as was true for Mallika Dutt, was visiting a friend in the hospital. Burks noticed one room had a warning sign on it and that nurses were drawing straws to see who would go in and check on the patient inside. Burks snuck into the room and found an emaciated man, close to death, asking to see his mother. No one was going to come see him, the nurses later told Burks, just as no one had come to see him in the six weeks he'd been in the hospital. That chance encounter propelled Burks into years of caring for men in similar situations, dying and alone. When no one else would, she stockpiled medications for them, tended them, and buried them. In the early days, she went to as many as three funerals a day.

Asked in interviews what propelled her to act, Burks credited God. She also identified a feeling of inevitability once she witnessed the suffering. "How could I not?" she said in a 2017 interview with *Arts & Understanding* magazine. "I feel people's suffering; animals, too. Sometimes it is hard to not reach out to everyone and to mind my own business. I had a rough childhood. My mom had TB and was in the hospital for a long time. My daddy took care of me during that time until he died. I was five. My mother wasn't equipped to be a mother, so I was on my own from an early age. I learned to just treat people like I wished someone had treated me."

Many, if not most, of those who stood up to this crisis were doing so from inside the afflicted communities. And they worked to counter helplessness with love. Burks recalled a scene she witnessed again and again. "I watched these men take care of their companions and watch them die," she said. "I've seen them go in and hold them up in the shower. They would hold them while I washed them. They would carry them back to the bed. We would dry them off and put lotion on them. They did that until the very end, knowing that they were going to be that person before long. Now, you tell me that's not love and devotion?"

Another considerable portion of the movement beyond helplessness was accomplished through anger-fueled protest, through insistence that the government change its policies, through screaming, "We count, too!" The AIDS Coalition to Unleash Power (ACT UP) is one of the best-known direct-action grassroots groups in this realm. Founded in Manhattan in the late 1980s, members of the group demonstrated for medical research, safe-sex education, and needle-exchange programs, and against denial of health insurance for people with HIV diagnoses and pharmaceutical company profiteering. I remember seeing the demonstrations, the sit-ins, all manner of civil disobedience in the late '80s. I remember the fierce intensity and determination emanating from the protestors. Anger and outrage spilled into the streets. AIDS is a case where silence really does mean death, the protestors asserted, and they refused to be silent.

HONORING THE MESSAGE OF THE ANGER

TO MY MIND, a counterproductive response to another person's anger would be to tell them to calm down. I would never try to make someone believe their anger is illegitimate. We feel what we feel. And the more we disparage the anger we feel, the more we try to tamp it down with shame or humiliation, the stronger it gets. I can't imagine talking to some of the people I talk to—a teacher whose student has been killed; a worker cheated out of hard-earned wages; someone whose right to walk down the street, or shop, or worship in safety is subverted; an elder whose intelligence and longing and innate dignity are routinely denied; the parent whose child has trouble breathing in an increasingly polluted world—and suggesting that person should push away their anger. The challenge lies in honoring the message of the anger without letting it consume us. Not because it is wrong to feel anger but because it might well burn us up.

Of course, there is no simple remedy for the outrages we face and the outrage we feel. But it's possible to forge a new relationship with our anger, relying on its conveyance of strength rather than its reactive quality. The strength is generated in a firm conviction about the innate dignity of all beings and the rightness of our universal wish to be happy. It's like a dialectic—we don't want to be lost in a fiery world that never lets us know peace, and we also don't want to be meek and afraid to take a stand. As the poet and novelist Maya Angelou said, "A wise woman wishes to be no one's enemy; a wise woman refuses to be anyone's victim."

Anger and outrage. It's in wrestling through these states that we may find the next foothold on the path to personal and global healing.

If we can be mindful with our anger, we can learn to use the energy and intelligence of it without getting lost in the tunnel vision it tends to foster. We're conditioned to turn away from anger or guilt, blame, jealousy, and so on. Feeling angry—at ourselves, at others, at experiences that come upon us—is undoubtedly intense, and we might fear that intensity will be all-consuming. So to avoid the rabbit hole of anger, our culture teaches us to find safety in repression. But there is a profound difference between recognizing anger for what it is and becoming lost in it.

In Buddhist psychology, they talk about transforming anger into discerning wisdom. Discerning wisdom is clarity, the willingness to let go of our assumptions and agendas to see more truthfully. It is the willingness to relinquish certain habits, like being a people pleaser or a perpetually defiant rebel, to have a more open, honest perception of a situation. Our habit of not wanting to rock the boat, for example, might lead us to hurriedly assert, "There's no problem here," while a more truthful view might state, "Big problem!" But in that transformation to discerning wisdom, we learn we can state a different view without the burning.

The founders of the Holistic Life Foundation (HLF), a Baltimore-based non-profit, have looked squarely at anger since they launched in 2001. HLF nurtures the wellness of children and adults in underserved communities by teaching yoga, mindfulness, and self-care. Its three founders are brothers Ali and Atman Smith, and Andrés González, whom the brothers met while all three attended the University of Maryland as undergrads. Since 2001, their work has spread to more than forty-two Baltimore-area schools, serving ten thousand people each week. While HLF's mission is to promote and spread love, they also acknowledge that anger plays a role.

"A lot of times anger gets a bad rap," Ali says. "We understand that you're not supposed to identify with that anger, but anger sometimes can be used to fuel people, you know? It doesn't have to be wrong that you're upset about something. There's a lot of things going on in the world that aren't cool, and that you get angry about. That's not a bad thing." The key, Ali says, is to not let it overwhelm you or stew in you so that you start lashing out; instead, he advocates using the anger to incite change.

"If people didn't get angry about a lot of things that occurred in the past, the world would be a much more screwed-up place right now than it already is. People got angry, they stood up for what they believed in, they made a stand, and they changed stuff. I think the problem is that some people go to screaming and yelling instead of understanding that you can use anger in a positive manner to make changes that are necessary in this world."

MINDFULNESS OF ANGER

THE GREAT IRONY is that the mere act of paying attention to anger through mindfulness can actually dissolve its toxicity and reduce the feeling of being overwhelmed by it. This idea is radically at odds with how we're taught to think about engaging with feelings like anger: either we think of anger as a fearful thing that needs to be repressed or as our only source of strength. Simply paying attention to it can be a difficult concept to grasp.

In my own teaching, students have often asked me if "paying attention to anger" involves trying to be cold, indifferent.

Absolutely not!

When you practice mindfulness of anger—when you feel it in your body, feel the complexity of it, the changing nature of it—you are working toward engaging with anger, and all the emotions and thoughts that arise, with presence and compassion. Then you can recognize the anger, capture the energy of it, and not fall into the fixation, bitterness, and greater hopelessness it can foster.

And so this week, in fact each and every week, I remind myself to breathe.

Rather than repeatedly resisting the anger, we can open up to the idea of practicing generosity with ourselves; we can simply allow the feeling to be there. By creating an environment of permission within, we release the expectation that painful states of mind like anger or depression or fear will consume us. They can arise, and we can let them go. It's a practice—of not holding on, of choosing *not* to identify, *not* to think, *This is who I am. This is who I will always be.* When we realize that these states are ever-changing, we can direct the forceful energy of anger in ways that are cleaner and stronger.

It takes profound willingness to shift this dynamic. When we do, we free ourselves from the habitual mind-set of meeting anger with a tight fist. We develop critical wisdom about our anger. We are no longer stuck in the idea that we have to meet hatred with hatred, that unthinking revenge is our only option, and instead, we realize the profound freedom we have to make a choice.

TAMING AND HARNESSING THE POWER

HEATHER YOUNTZ IS a Boston lawyer who focuses mainly on immigration cases and has had to deal with immigrant children being incarcerated separately from their parents. The legal world is a highly stressful arena, an adversarial system where anger can be a real challenge, but most lawyers seem to regard anger as an essential emotion in the fight for justice. Heather told us that when she was younger,

> My anger scared me. I didn't know how to harness it, and it would become something that would often start one way and then end up out of control. With experience, though,

I have found that anger is a focusing emotion for me, and I can use it well to make my points in rapid succession. If I'm in court and I'm angry about what's happening, I find I'm sharper in some ways. Anger is like holding a hose that's running on full blast. If you're able to hold on to it, you're doing great. But the second you loosen your grip, it just goes all over the place.

When anger has taken me over, I can have a problem sleeping, especially in the last few years, when my work has become even more intense. When my three-year-old daughter woke me up recently at three o'clock in the morning, she went right back to sleep, but then as I crawled back in my own bed, I had this image of one of the children we'd been working with who was separated from her parents, and she was woken up in the middle of the night by a customs and border protection officer yanking on her braid, her ponytail, screaming, "It's time to take a shower!" That image just flashed, and that was it. I could not get back to sleep. That's an example of the anger having power over me in a way that makes life difficult. But I have to find ways to work with it, and one of the best for me is exercise. I have an elliptical machine in my house, and sometimes I'm so frustrated with my job when I get home, I go straight upstairs and get on the elliptical and put on dance music and just bang it out. I'm also very careful with drinking and anger. That can be a slippery slope. If I'm about to have a drink, I ask myself if I'm doing it because I'm feeling frustrated with my life right now or for enjoyment? I have found that there is definitely a difference.

What I've seen in my own experience and in the experience of others is that there are powerful and important elements in anger that can be extracted to serve rather than rule us. When you strip away the fear/aggression/territoriality/destructiveness/ domination from anger, you have *insight* (clearly seeing, for example, that something is very wrong or that someone has been deeply wronged or harmed) and *energy*, which together take the form of courage. You can act and stand your ground, skillfully, since neither is based on the polarity of trying to obliterate someone else. The sense of discerning right and wrong remains, the sense of urgency may remain, but it is all laced through with compassion—for ourselves as well as others.

HARNESSING THE ENERGY OF ANGER

AUTHOR, ACTIVIST, AND political strategist Marc Solomon came out of the closet as a gay man in the late 1990s. He was, he told me, dealing with a barrage of emotions at the time. A little while later, he came to a lovingkindness retreat I led, still feeling emotional turmoil. He said:

> After coming out, I was just feeling so much rage. The retreat was a groundbreaking experience for me. It felt like it was the first time I saw that I really had the ability to direct love and to feel love toward myself and toward others in a bold and honest way, and it really changed my life. That's when I decided I was going [to] leave graduate school, throw all my stuff in storage, and take a year off. I backpacked across the West and meditated for a year. Soon after that, I started my activism work on marriage equality.

Picking up Marc's story at the end of his year of self-exploration, it's impressive to see how those challenging feelings of rage that he could have drowned in alcohol, he instead alchemized into something powerfully action-oriented:

> Eventually, I could see more clearly through the cobwebs, and what shined most brightly was how passionate I was about making the world better for LGBTQ kids. I found deep compassion for LGBTQ young people . . . and for myself as a young person. I didn't want young people to have to struggle with their sexuality in the ways that I did. A deep sense of connectedness and purpose was one of the things I got from meditation—and continue to get from meditation. We are not alone, we all are looking to be happy and fulfilled, and there's lots of compassion to go around.

The mechanics of casting anger into an appropriate, productive role can be challenging to master, but fortunately, there are people in the world dedicated to breaking open this sometimes-mysterious process. I'm inspired by those, like all whom I've mentioned, who work to harness the energy of anger instead of succumbing to it. This is not a casual or leisurely task. I've found it demands vision and a strong commitment to not simply yield to the immediate satisfaction of raging at what is so manifestly unjust or cruel.

Another person who exemplifies this ability to reframe anger is Roshi Francisco "Paco" Genkoji Luagoviña. Paco is an unstoppable community organizer, activist, and ordained Buddhist priest (among other things). Now in his eighties, Paco gladly tells people that he's never completely flushed away his anger . . . and he doesn't expect to anytime soon. He is a man who recognizes his own outrage. He tells me:

I still got anger in me. I'm angry about the injustices. I'm angry about the injustice and disrespect dealt to Puerto Rico for many years. I really get pissed off. I say, "I'll be angry until I die." But I also say, "I don't define myself as an angry man." It's an emotion in me. I'll say, "Okay, let's see what we can do. Oh, anger! There you are. There you are, let's have some coffee. Let's see what we can do: Why don't we start some demonstrations at Ralph Bunche Plaza in the UN? Let's get a couple of people." So we've been going to Ralph Bunche Plaza every two weeks, and the first time, it was just three of us. The second time, it was seven of us. And next Saturday, there will probably be a hundred of us. That's how I use anger.

A BIGGER PERSPECTIVE

TO MEET AND work through our anger calls for discernment and compassion, yes, but it also calls for a broadened perspective.

How do we get perspective?

How do we experience anger in a bigger, even immense, framework?

How do we transmute it to a more steadfast, courageous energy?

For some, it is awareness of death itself that brings perspective. As we connect to the inevitable end of life, tabulating wins and losses often doesn't seem the point. Instead, we tend to reflect on whether we have been wholehearted or not, fully present for our lives and our efforts or not. Paco talks about the radical openness he learned by sitting at people's deathbeds:

> I take lessons from the people who work with death and dying, which has always been a fascination for me even before I became a Zen Buddhist priest—the holy show of life and death. When you're at somebody's deathbed and they're still conscious and they still talk, you've got to sit there being present, with no expectations. Because every death, every person, every situation is so absolutely different, if you go with preconceived notions about anything, you miss the point. You need to hold somebody's hand and just be there. And whatever emerges is whatever it is.

I always find it helpful to realize and remember that we can only do what we can do, even if we won't be around to see the outcome of our efforts—what Lin-Manuel Miranda calls "planting seeds in a garden you never get to see." I remember standing at Yad Vashem, the Holocaust memorial in Jerusalem, where the anguish of the Holocaust—the deaths, the destruction, the cruelty—is so clearly evidenced. All I could think was, *Some things are more than a one-generation fix.* Now, as I bring to mind that thought, something inside me relaxes—not into indolence or complacency but into a steadier effort that isn't in an impossible hurry.

Sometimes we find ourselves confronting a seemingly intractable problem. We're overwhelmed and don't know what to do to make it all okay . . . until, after a time, we realize we need to do the one small thing that's in front of us, or nothing will ever change. We sit and remember we are worth something—that all of us are—and we use that realization to give us courage and determination.

The understanding of some things likely being more than a one-generation fix resurfaced for me vividly when I was talking to a friend who lives in Paris. A white man born in France, he was dismayed by his encounter that day with a group of young people. They seemed to be ethnically North African, and he knew that many people that age, in that demographic, were born or brought up in France. They were hanging out on the streets, taunting him and cursing his parents as he walked by. He was both frightened and contemptuous. Later, as we were having the conversation, he mused a bit and then put the interaction into a larger context. "Many of them probably have parents who translated for the French in countries like Algeria," my friend supposed. "Those parents were promised the earth were they to come to France, but then they came to France and were given nothing, often treated very poorly." The wrongs of colonialism weren't going to disappear overnight or in one generation, he commented. As we finished speaking, he said that it felt important for him to try to remember that larger perspective and to respond to situations in a way that included it.

When we are forced to acknowledge that some things are not a one-generation fix, we could easily end up at apathy or hopelessness. Instead, I've found that it's possible for the perspective this realization affords to allow me to more fully honor the complexity, intricacy, and poignancy of the pain I witness. It doesn't oversimplify it or compartmentalize it. It's an honest view, and it fortifies my determination to keep working toward a better world.

Marc Solomon shared with me that in his experience over a

long career of activism including fifteen years on marriage equality, "the people who get big things done are people with staying power." He added that

> Jumping into a cause and focusing on it for a couple of years isn't enough, because if you're trying to do something big, it's going to take time to figure out how to do it, and figure out how to make the case. And then it still might take a long time before you see any concrete change. My mentor, Evan Wolfson, wrote his thesis at Harvard Law School in 1983 on why gay people should be able to marry, and he didn't see any gay person get married in the U.S. for more than twenty years after that. You're going to have losses and setbacks along the way, so it's important to have a clear vision of what you're trying to create, one that syncs up with your deepest priorities and aspirations. It also helps to relish smaller victories even while keeping your eyes on the prize. My job working for marriage equality was to put points on the board every single day in some positive way. That could mean getting a good editorial in *The New York Times* or *The Boston Globe,* or getting a new unexpected person who supports the cause to speak about it publicly. Those were important building blocks to getting a statewide marriage equality law passed while also giving us the affirmation that we were moving in the right direction.

It would be easy for someone like Marc, working on a slow and multigenerational effort to change the world, to succumb to hopelessness and powerlessness, leading to an anger that festers. It would be easy for any of us with our daily struggle to bring about change in some way. And yet, as we saw with so many people in this chapter, when you investigate anger with curiosity and love, when you actually listen and pay attention—not getting embroiled in either the burning energy or the fighting—you can ask, "Is there something in here? Is there something in this situation that is good or useful even though it's not all breaking the way I would like?"

When we simply listen to anger or outrage, it has the potential to become a source of enormous energy. When we feel the anger directly, learn it in our bodies, look at the pain at the heart of it, get some space around it through perspective-building and openness, and steadily leaven it with compassion for ourselves and others, then we can mine its energy and use that as courage. The kind of courage that makes it possible to act in the face of no immediate visible outcome. The kind of courage that lets you sit with not knowing what to do, that frees you to do the small thing that's in front of you. Remember that you are worth something. Remember that we all are. Use that knowledge as your North Star.

PRACTICE: DIFFICULT THOUGHTS AND EMOTIONS

WE CAN PRACTICE being with difficult emotions and thoughts, even intense ones, in an open, allowing, and accepting way. For many of us, this is the opposite of the more automatic mode of pushing away uncomfortable feelings out of fear or annoyance, or doing everything we can to avoid painful experiences, at whatever cost.

Very commonly when something unpleasant happens, we project it into a seemingly unchanging future: *This is going to last forever. This is never going to change. Things will always be this way.*

Or we might have the habit of creating a whole self-image around it: *I'm a bad person. I'm a bad mother because this unwelcome thought is happening in my mind right now.*

What we're doing in this meditation practice is looking at the difference between what is actually happening in the moment, even if it's difficult, and what we add to it in terms of future projection, or unfairly blaming ourselves, or feeling we should be in control of what arises in our minds, or creating a solid self-image out of something that is actually impermanent—all of which can add to the stress and challenge we experience. In our practice, we look for these add-ons and see if we can let them go.

We can't stop a thought or emotion from arising. No one can. But we can be empowered by our ability to relate to thoughts and emotions in a whole new way—learning not to buy into them while at the same time not unfairly blaming ourselves for what no one at all can keep from arising.

We can have a whole new sense of space and also some kindness toward ourselves when these difficult things arise.

You can begin this practice by bringing to mind a difficult or troubling thought or situation—some situation that carries for you intense emotion, such as sadness, fear, shame, or anger.

See where you feel it in your body. What does it feel like? Where do you feel sensations arising? How are these sensations changing? Can you experience them fully in the present moment without getting highjacked by them or without immediately or anxiously working to make them go away?

If you see those kinds of reactions in your mind, settle back, come back into your body, feel the different sensations being born of that emotion in this moment.

If you find you are adding judgment, condemnation, future projection—anything like that—practice letting go of those reactions, as best you can, almost as though they were birds flying out of your hands into the air. Then return to the simple sensations of the emotion, absent the add-ons.

Bring your focus of awareness to the part of the body where those sensations are the strongest. Once your attention has moved to the bodily sensations, perhaps say to yourself, *It's okay. Whatever it is, it's okay. I can feel this without pushing it away or getting caught up in it.* Staying with the awareness of the bodily sensations and your relationship to them, accepting them, letting them be, softening and opening to them.

Often, the emotion is not just one thing. It may be moments of sadness, moments of fear, moments of frustration, moments of helplessness. Just watch them rise and pass away. None of these states is permanent, unchanging. They're moving, changing, shifting.

No matter what story or add-on arises, come back to your direct experience in the moment: "What am I feeling right now? What's its nature?"

It may be that the painful situation is coming mostly in the form of thoughts. As a habit, certain thought patterns arise that we tend to get lost in, overcome by, defined by, even as we resent or fear them. We can retrain our whole mental attitude by first learning to recognize these patterns, and perhaps even calmly naming them: "Oh, here is the pattern of thinking, *Everything is wrong,* the pattern of thinking, *I'm a failure,* the pattern of thinking,

Nothing will ever change." Once we recognize them, we can remind ourselves these are just visiting, they are not essentially who we are, we couldn't stop them from visiting, but we can let them go.

After you finish this formal session of practice, you can explore bringing into your everyday life this consideration: "What am I feeling right now? Am I pushing away or being carried off by emotion or thought?" Return again and again to this moment.

4

GRIEF TO RESILIENCE

✳

T HE BUDDHA POINTED OUT THOUSANDS of years ago that suffering is a fact of life. Or, as I occasionally put it: *Some things just hurt*. I have jokingly said that I want that as my epitaph, or at least to have a mug or a T-shirt with that slogan emblazoned across it while I'm still alive.

SOME THINGS
JUST HURT

There are those who assert that if only we didn't try to resist our experience, or have a bad attitude, there would be no pain at all. I challenge that. It's inevitable that by simply living a life, there will be times of adversity and certainly disruption. It's not because of our attitude that those times are uncomfortable or heartbreaking. And for the dedicated many who work to make their community or the world at large a kinder, more insightful place, the suffering they aim to alleviate will often spill into their own lives. You may be one of them. That experience of vicarious trauma—which we can also call the *shock of witnessing*—has all sorts of repercussions: post-traumatic stress disorder (PTSD), burnout, depression, and despair among them. While I believe it's true that some things just hurt, I also believe that we don't need *extra* suffering, and therein lies our work. How do we fully acknowledge the suffering but at the same time not let it define and overtake us?

For a start, it helps to recognize that for many of us, a dominant cultural attitude toward pain is that it's something to be avoided, denied, "treated." As a result, it can be particularly tough for people—including me—to acknowledge painful emotions in the context of our efforts toward growth and transformation and social change. Some of us may feel that the cultivation of compassion should be a practice that elevates us beyond feeling those "less virtuous" emotions like anger, annoyance, impatience, and disappointment. But part of the cultivation of compassion is simple recognition—including the recognition of those things that just hurt.

That's why the revolutionary statement that there is suffering in the world is so liberating. It doesn't turn away or include a prescription of precisely how we should feel in those times when we suffer. In fact, the most radical part of this piece of wisdom is its simplicity; it is merely recognition of what is. When I first encountered the idea of the truth of suffering in an Asian philosophy class in college, I felt instantly comforted, and the comfort was unlike anything I'd experienced before. No one was trying to make sense of my pain or rationalize it; no one was reassuring me that things would get better soon or reminding me to look only at the bright side—all things we are conditioned to say and believe in the face of suffering. For the first time, I felt permission and freedom to feel whatever I was going to feel.

RECOGNITION AND ACKNOWLEDGMENT

AT TIMES, PAIN can reach such a powerful level that it can be devastating. In spiritual life, we might call it the *dark night of the soul*. In interpersonal life, we call it *grief,* and this intense emotional experience does not limit itself to the loss of someone who has died. It can occur as the experience of nearly any kind of deep loss. I learned that in a poignant way from a man who was deeply suffering.

A young soldier who had been deployed in Iraq came to IMS within two weeks of having been released from the army. He was a beautiful person. He had enlisted for a few different reasons: a recent romantic heartbreak, a yearning to get out of town, and deeply felt ideals about love of country. Not only had he landed in an active war zone, he had also experienced massive disillusionment and real horror at actions he witnessed. I had never met someone in as active a state of traumatic distress as he was, outside of an actual traumatic situation occurring on the spot. His startle reflex was extraordinary; he lived on tenterhooks. His need to take measures to feel safe was absolute. His incredibly sweet nature did regular battle with his mistrust and persistent monitoring of others.

The intensive, silent retreat he'd signed up for wouldn't have been the ideal environment to begin processing that recent experience, so we worked with him on a parallel track—more relational, emphasizing grounding exercises and especially self-compassion.

His later diagnosis was PTSD, but it could equally have been described as moral injury or a soul wound. The lead teacher of the retreat he entered was my colleague Rodney Smith, who had also founded and run two hospices. I was talking to Rodney about the soldier one day when he said to me, "Sharon, don't you see? He's grieving."

Once I understood his mistrust and hypervigilance and alienation as grief, it registered within me as heartbreak, which I, too, have often felt. His pain didn't seem as distant as a diagnosis like PTSD. Consequently, I was better able to be a friend and teacher to him.

To grieve, whether for a person, a set of ideals, or our hopes and dreams, is to watch reality, once so solid-seeming, become molten. It's hard to get oneself to take the next step in a dissolving world—where will our foot land when it seems nothing will support us? How do we move toward inner or outer change?

To start with, here are some footholds for our next step, thanks to two insightful writers.

"Grief expressed out loud for someone we have lost, or a country or home we have lost, is in itself the greatest praise we could ever give them," says writer Martín Prechtel. "Grief is praise, because it is the natural way love honors what it misses." Seeing grief in this way helps us respect what we are going through, rather than being mired in shame and discouragement on top of the pain we already feel.

What happens if we recognize the love inside of grief? Journalist Dahr Jamail writes about his grief for the planet on Truthout, a nonprofit news website:

> Each time another scientific study is released showing yet another acceleration of the loss of ice atop the Arctic Ocean, or sea-level-rise projections are stepped up yet again, or news that another species has gone extinct is announced, my heart breaks for what we have done and are doing to the planet. . . .
>
> Grieving for what is happening to the planet also now brings me gratitude for the smallest, most mundane things. Grief is also a way to honor what we are losing. . . . My acceptance of our probable decline opens into a more intimate and heartfelt union with life itself. The price of this opening is the repeated embracing of my own grief. . . . I am grieving and yet I have never felt more alive. I have found that it's possible to reach a place of acceptance and inner peace, while enduring the grief and suffering that are inevitable as the biosphere declines.

THE NEED FOR RESILIENCE

AN ACTIVIST I greatly admire is the late Myles Horton. Among other accomplishments, he co-founded the Highlander Folk School, a center for education and social action now known as the Highlander Research and Education Center. Horton established Highlander in 1932, when he was in his late twenties, and by the 1960s, it had evolved into a site for leadership training for advocates of civil rights, labor, voting rights, and the environment. Early on, Horton determined that Highlander would operate as a racially integrated institution; he claimed that by doing so, it held the record for sustained civil disobedience, breaking the Tennessee Jim Crow laws every day for over forty years, until the segregation laws were finally repealed.

In the 1985 documentary *You Got to Move,* Horton shared the outlook that sustained him: "I think the future is . . . well, as somebody said one time, 'It's out there.' But it's not only out there; it's ready to be changed. It's malleable, and there's nothing fixed that you can't unfix. But to unfix things that appear to be fixed, you have to not only be creative and imaginative, but courageously dedicated to the long haul."

Social justice activist Chenjerai Kumanyika wrote about resilience from his experiences of working for change: "I've seen so many people and coalitions break down partially due to an inability to detach from the brutal vicissitudes of passing moments. I myself have foolishly tried to stand like a rigid oak against the winds of struggle, failing to bend and dance where necessary. The fights we need to fight are long and we have to sustain our capacity."

Creating change requires enduring energy, but so much can get in the way of that energy. Therefore, it's helpful for each of us to explore the landscapes of our lives and try to discover what comes between us and that long haul.

How do we lose energy? For one thing, we get overwhelmed in our own feelings of loss or grief or pain. We become rigid, like that oak, instead of bending and dancing where necessary. We demand perfection of ourselves in this highly imperfect world, and we don't honor the fact that maybe we can take only one step at a time. We feel our bodies changing, our emotions become unstable—rapidly cycling through one mood after another. Relationships fade, goals recede, we are pressured to perform, pressured to stand out, pressured to disappear. We try so hard to help someone, and it seems like it's going nowhere or taking longer than forever. Can we beat the clock ticking away, marking entropy and despair? Sometimes the thought goes through my head, *I'm so tired I could cry.* Sometimes I am so tired I do cry.

Many of us are familiar with the spectrum of depletion: we just can't catch up, we feel overwhelmed and exhausted, we no longer find meaning in what we're doing, we burn out, or we are actively traumatized as we absorb the trauma of those we work with or live with or deeply care about.

Emmett Fitzgerald is an Irishman who grew up in London. At age twenty-five, he deployed to the war-torn Congo to do humanitarian aid work. Despite how intense and unsettling the work was, Emmett kept re-upping, returning to Congo again and again for six-month tours. For the next chapter of his life, when the 2010 earthquake devastated Haiti, he went there to run a camp for displaced persons and ended up dealing with local storms that wrecked the camp and prompted an outbreak of cholera. Emmett just kept diving into disaster after disaster, almost like a "disaster tourist," he said, but all the while putting his emotional life on hold. When he would travel from home to his next tour, he said, "I'd be visualizing a cardboard box and I would put the emotional stuff, the relationship stuff, the personal stuff in it and then that would be put away while I was in work mode. I found it very hard to align the two pieces of myself."

Eventually, after Haiti, Emmett collapsed.

I lost a bunch of weight. I was smoking for the first time in my life, and I got back [to London] and found that I really had a taste for whiskey even though it had never been my thing. I now had a taste for sitting alone in my apartment smoking cigarettes and listening to music and just not wanting to engage in any effort. I didn't want to be in the same room with anyone. That was frightening because I'd missed everybody so much. And then, the panic attacks started. I had one on Christmas Day in my parents' home. I was surrounded by my big Irish family, by everybody I love, on my favorite day of the year, and yet I found myself deliberately excusing myself from the room, trying to be away from people because I couldn't stand the effort of being sociable—trying to be what my family remembered me as and expected me to be. The amount of control it was taking to be in the room was so much that I would just need to release it. I couldn't be surrounded by everybody I loved. My heart was racing. I could hear the blood in my fucking ears. It was cacophonous. It was like trying to have a conversation and being screamed at, at the same time.

When we are in the darkest night of our soul, grieving for the person and the life we seem to have lost, at that point we need to acknowledge what is, not how we would prefer it or what we would settle for. This is how things are, despite our protestations or laments or great yearning to look the other way.

Emmett began to discover resilience after he found his way to yoga and mindfulness. "You're thinking it's all your fault and you need to be able to deal with this on your own," he said, "then a yoga and mindfulness teacher releases the pressure. It was a little shaft of sunlight. A little moment of clarity in your head and the anxiety stops. Meditation just helped me to acknowledge and just sit with how I was feeling and not constantly try to change it or do something that would justify it."

WHAT HAS HAPPENED HAS HAPPENED

I WAS ATTENDING a talk of the Dalai Lama's on an early anniversary of 9/11, that day in 2001 that marked the largest terrorist attack on American soil in history. I had known people who died in the Twin Towers. I was in New York City within a week of the attack and stayed there for two months to teach. Several people came to my classes right from volunteering at ground zero. I will never forget the look of pain in their eyes as they came in to lean, exhausted, against a pillar. Through the meditation and with one another, several told me privately, they longed to find something beautiful that had not been destroyed.

During his remarks, His Holiness the Dalai Lama said something that could be easily misunderstood or seen as overly simplistic but which had a profound impact on me. He said, "About 9/11. It happened."

Hearing that, I felt a sense of relief, like something awry had just clicked into place. I already recognized 9/11 had happened, certainly. But with any traumatic event, we might well need time to more fully integrate, in body, mind, and spirit that "it happened." It's easy, along the way, to want to overexplain a shattering situation or take refuge in abstractions. With the Dalai Lama's statement, I dropped a subtle tendency to interpret or try to fabricate what I was feeling—and more directly recognized what was simply true for me.

In a similar spirit, Zen teacher Roshi Joan Halifax cautions against trying to convince ourselves to regard childhood traumas as gifts. She suggests, "Think of them as givens, not gifts." That way there's no pretense or pressure to reimagine painful experiences. If something is a given, we don't deny it or look the other way. We start by acknowledging it, then see how we can make the best life possible going forward.

Lynn Nottage, the playwright we met in chapter 1, talks about a breakthrough coming for her when, as she said during a public dialogue we had in New York City a few years ago:

> I had to go inside of myself in ways I was not prepared to do and confront my own sadness and my own sense of loss, and then figure out a way to translate those emotions to the page. I chose to do it through metaphor, but it was a very difficult process. I describe it as being like that moment in [the film] *Like Water for Chocolate* when the young woman is preparing dinner and all of her tears are mixing with the ingredients, and when people finally eat the food, they can't help but be overcome with emotion because they recognize something that's truthful in those flavors.

BUILDING RESILIENCE

THIS ACKNOWLEDGMENT OF the need to truly touch our sadness, pain, and loss is where real change is born, where we begin to build resilience. As we respond to our own pain with more presence and compassion, the energy we have for responding to the pain of others increases dramatically, as does our sense of connection and care.

Resilience is something that accretes over time as we develop a habit of courageously responding to or being with pain without freaking out. At some point, you notice you bend but don't break. In fact, even mighty oaks can bend in the wind without breaking. After Samantha Novick suffered the Parkland shooting, as we saw earlier, she described it as a giant crater, a gaping hole in everyone's lives. Over time, through working with others, "having a clear purpose, meditating, spending time with her family, and in nature," and having a renewed sense of the preciousness of life, that hole in her life, which will never disappear, is nevertheless not as big.

In working to make change in the world, there will always be setbacks. We have to be able to get back up off the floor. We need to be able to bounce back. Sure, we get caught up in the heat of the moment or in a sense of failure or are attracted to the shiny object that grabs our attention, but then we start over. If you come at an effort toward change with great rigidity, then any challenge feels like the end of the story, and you're sunk.

I was working with a physical therapist recently, and one of the exercises he had me do was to stand on one foot. When I did, I would teeter, or sway, or my hand would reach out to grab the countertop in front of me. The physical therapist loved this! "Look at how your body is working to recover balance," he'd say. "That's the really important part." Instead of seeing all that wobbling as a failure, he saw it as an essential skills training—my body recapturing the intelligence of how to come back to balance. That was more important than doing the exercise perfectly. "Good job!" he'd exclaim.

Joel Daniels, the storyteller/activist who wrote *A Book About Things I Will Tell My Daughter*, talked to me about how to cultivate resilience in the face of frustration:

For me, it starts with being able to relate to how I respond to the world. And I need to recognize that I'm not always going to respond with love. Sometimes I respond by being a dick. And I have to remind myself to forgive myself for not responding in the way I feel I should. What's really helped, though—it always does—is coming back to the breath. It's the foundation I can work from: I can lean back into it and go, "Okay, in this present moment in time, this is the way that I know I need to respond because I've been here before."

The older I've gotten, the more I've been able to lean into being vulnerable, because it feels most honest to me. I see pain for what it is. I'm resting with it. I acknowledge it. I'm a next-door neighbor with it. I know this pain is eventually going to move away.

SUFFERING AND CREATIVITY

IN 2010, I attended a discussion at Emory University with panelists, including the Dalai Lama, called "The Creative Journey: Artists in Conversation with the Dalai Lama on Spirituality and Creativity."

The first question for the panel was: "In the West, many people believe that creativity comes from torment, while in the East, there is more of a tradition of great art coming from balance and realization. Do you think you have to be in great suffering to create great art?"

I have been asked that question countless times, for many years and in many places. I've seen well-known painters sit in intensive meditation retreats, all the while quite torn about being there because they feared the end result would be losing their edge. I've seen writers equate balance with dullness and peace with torpor. I've known actors and musicians who feared ease of heart because that seemed to them the last step before being asleep.

The Dalai Lama had quite an interesting response to the question. In his view, beautiful art was beautiful because of the inner transformation artists went through during the act of creation. Had they become more enlightened, kinder, more deeply aware? To him, that's what made a poem or a sculpture or painting more valuable, worthy of being held in higher esteem.

Because I think of making art as social action, I began to wonder whether the same principle could be applied to caregivers or those seeking societal transformation. What if we could regard our lives—our bodies and minds and work—as our fundamental creative medium?

This is a very different view of creativity from one that posits that all great art needs to come from immense torment and suffering. What I think we actually want (and rely on) from those in creative or transformational roles is not their misery. It is their courage: the courage to break through boundaries, to see things differently, daring to not conform.

As Lynn Nottage has said, "Great art comes from the truth. There's a difference between a piece of art that is impeccably crafted because the artists are skilled technicians—the work may be beautiful but somehow it doesn't move you—and a piece of art where the lines may be a little sloppy but there is an undeniable truth reflected back. It becomes great art not because it is perfect but because the artist has successfully conveyed their own truth."

Suffering may bring some of us to that place of courage and truth, for sure, but so, too, might a profound connection to another or to life itself. When we aren't so lost in the grasping and craving and mindless consumerism and aimless competition that conventional society invites, we can step away from the dictates of the ordinary to see and express reality in a fresh way.

Tasmanian comedian Hannah Gadsby creates performances that exemplify the connection between art and social change. In her remarkable monologue *Nanette,* she talks about Vincent van Gogh and offers up the theory that we don't have the painting *Sunflowers* because of his brokenness, his mental anguish. We have *Sunflowers* because Van Gogh and his brother Theo loved each other. "Through all of the pain [Vincent] had a tether, a connection to the world," she says. The art was born of connection.

As a society, we're phobic about looking at pain, but it's also true that happiness can seem superficial, a mere escape rather than something fundamental. Through practices like generosity and lovingkindness, which lift your spirits, you can come to look at pain without being overcome by it. You're not destroyed by it. You have more spaciousness, more lift. That ability to face pain without crumbling is sometimes seen as the same as being oblivious or being protected by privilege. I see it as a profound potential of the human heart.

AVOIDING THE EXTREMES: GLORIFYING OR DENYING

IN THE BUDDHIST tradition, suffering is not considered redemptive; it does not equal grace. Everything depends on how we relate to that suffering, our attitude: we may emerge embittered and isolated and self-absorbed, or connected and caring and not feeling alone. One ingredient in a transformed relationship to pain is to have enough light to surround the darkness, openness big enough to hold the pain and not collapse into it. A heart as wide as the world. Suffering *is,* it hurts, and yet we have the capacity to not add shame, or rage at not being able to control it, or conviction we will never feel anything else, ever.

My colleague Sylvia Boorstein tells a funny story about her granddaughter Honor. While preparing for their Passover Seder, Sylvia asked then-nine-year-old Honor to help set the table and gave her the following instructions: "Take a teaspoon of horseradish and put it on top of each piece of gefilte fish."

Honor agreed to follow the instructions, but didn't hesitate to offer her personal reaction to the traditional Seder menu item: "I never knew you could take a truly terrible thing and make it even worse!"

If we can put aside the fact that Sylvia makes delicious gefilte fish and the fact that I love horseradish, Honor's comment could be used to illustrate how many of us deal with difficult feelings.

When we feel like we're experiencing a truly terrible thing, we often don't let the feeling exist on its own. Instead, we make it worse. Perhaps we judge ourselves for not being able to let go of the negative feeling; perhaps we ruminate extensively about the past and stew in regret or guilt; perhaps we allow ourselves to start projecting into the future, convinced the pain will never go away or even abate. Regardless of the details of the situation or the particulars of how we make it worse for ourselves, this is a common reaction coming from the sheer force of our conditioning.

This is why meditation can help to alleviate suffering. Despite popular myths, meditation doesn't cleanse us of thoughts and feelings, but it does support us in having a more direct relationship to our experiences. For some, meditation is most supportive simply because it enables us to become more aware of the source of our pain. As a result, we rely less on reactions like denial, self-judgment, or precariously looking for happiness in transitory places. By experiencing suffering more directly, yet stepping back from being overwhelmed, we can learn to respond to our situations thoughtfully, rather than react immediately.

As the CEO of the END Fund, Ellen Agler is someone who has to make many hard decisions in the midst of great suffering. The END Fund is devoted to controlling and eliminating neglected tropical diseases (NTDs). NTDs are a group of infectious diseases, such as river blindness and intestinal worms, that affect more than 1.5 billion people globally, including over 800 million children.

Ellen said to me that she tries to take a step back before making big decisions. "It's okay to pause before responding," she said. "It's okay to just be with what is and see how it might be a different 'what is,' if you just wait a day or two and try to access wisdom and see a deeper truth that may be what really needs to be responded to."

Ellen's comment parallels so much of what meditation training offers: the ability to pause rather than rush headlong into action, the opening of space so we can see options perhaps hidden from us in the ordinary clutter of our reactiveness, the greater ability to be with the suffering we feel without recoiling from it.

Accepting suffering doesn't mean it will disappear. Instead, we can learn to feel discomfort in a far purer and more direct way, without the additional burden of feeling humiliated by it. A woman who recently underwent a major loss asked me for advice, as she was feeling pressured by friends to get better, to let go of the anguish, to heal. Their impatience was making her feel entirely alienated from them; she was convinced her suffering made her fundamentally different. "My friends have golden lives," she insisted. I didn't believe that for a moment, knowing how much goes on behind closed doors and how much pressure there is in today's world to present as "perfect." Hearing her describe her tough situation, these words spilled out of my mouth: "I think you need new friends. Maybe you need to meet mine. They're all wrecks!"

I don't really think my friends are wrecks. I do think, however, that they and I tend to talk more directly about our suffering, whether it stems from family issues, work stress, or free-floating anxiety . . . the list goes on. It's the self-critical add-ons we layer onto pain that make us struggle terribly in response to tough situations. This perspective makes an enemy of our suffering, when dealing with the pain itself can already feel like quite a lot.

Social entrepreneur Anurag Gupta, founder of Be More America, deliberated about his journey to a more workable relationship with suffering:

> Starting when I was in law school, for about ten years, I spent at least thirty days every year in silent retreats. I did that because I felt so judgmental of myself. As someone who was an advocate for social change in impoverished and marginalized communities, who was also coming from a place of woundedness, I was very much out of my body. I was in my head, which was creating a lot of judgments. Immersing myself in the practice of yoga has led to grounding. So regardless of whatever the stories, the mythologies, the biases that are out there about what my body is supposed to be—its color, size, background—I was at least able to experience real embodiment.

ASKING HARD QUESTIONS:
GETTING TO THE ROOT

SOME YEARS BACK, I was invited to participate in a gathering of close to fifty Buddhists and Christians that took place at the Cistercian (Trappist) Abbey of Gethsemani in Kentucky. The Dalai Lama suggested and encouraged this unique meeting of monks, nuns, and other practitioners, and he proposed the site as well. (It had been the Trappist monk Thomas Merton's monastery.)

The first few days were cordial, well intentioned but awkward. Dignitaries from both religions read out their lists of monastics who were going to make extended visits to their counterparts' monasteries or nunneries to learn something of the other tradition up close. The Dalai Lama insisted on being treated like any other monk and so came down off his throne and sat among the people. We chatted with him during tea—that was an unexpected treat.

But apart from that, the dialogue was formal, exceedingly polite, and somehow not igniting much passion, which was odd given that most people in that room had passion enough to commit decades of their lives to Buddhism or Christianity. This went on until one of the participants, Zen teacher Norman Fischer, posed this question: "Now that I am in this monastery, when I see all the crosses with the figure of Jesus on them, I find it quite sad. The cross itself I do not find sad, but when there is a figure of Jesus on the cross, I find that quite sad. And so I want to ask the question, and I mean this very sincerely: Do you Christian participants feel sad, too, when you see this? And how do you practice with this image? I would really be interested to know."

Norman struck me as a particularly guileless person—he wasn't trying to be provocative, but really was troubled at the sight of the crucifix and was struggling to understand. In the face of his sincerity, whole walls came crashing down. There was a broad spectrum of responses, but in each response there was a common thread—that of sitting face-to-face with the truth of suffering.

People were so eager to address the topic, they began talking over one another. Some spoke of the "demons" within that one faces during contemplative practice. Some spoke of their intense frustration with tradition-bound hierarchies. Some Buddhists spoke about living in exile and cultural dislocation. (One Tibetan monk felt comfortable enough to bemusedly ask, "Is it true you believe in some kind of original sin?")

Some Christians spoke of their shock and horror when colleagues were murdered while working overseas. Finally, we were actually recognizing ourselves in one another, finally, we were willing to be vulnerable and truthful and offer our deepest faith and our honest uncertainty and our unacknowledged fear, and it all came from *openly talking about suffering*. The dialogue we had come together in Kentucky to have, it turned out, was about this.

The dialogue became about sitting face-to-face with that truth and not turning away, however much we wanted to, not strategizing for a quick fix to cover over the pain and not adorning it with romance or ballads or glitter. Suffering hurts, and here we are.

THE INTIMACY OF PAIN

IN AN INTERVIEW for this book, Michael Kink, an advocate for a fairer economy, talks about finding his way through suffering and grief:

My practice began because I was an out-of-control alcoholic. I went to a program where they encourage you to use meditation as part of your recovery from alcoholism and drug addiction. So my meditation practice has literally always been grounded in this community of people of wildly diverse backgrounds. What has helped me with grieving is just having the perspective that suffering is part of life, and that it's not a separation of life, and that our practices in our communities are intended to allow us to hold suffering as part of our human experience. Before I came to Buddhism, I knew suffering was part of life, but I had not acknowledged it at the deepest level as part of what we have and who we are.

When we are honest about pain, we see, as so many in this chapter have said, that it is a deep and inevitable part of life, an ever-recurring companion, and there is no immediate fix. But we also find that we are not alone.

During a panel discussion at the 2019 Wisdom 2.0 conference, Fred Guttenberg, whose daughter, Jaime, was killed at Marjory Stoneman Douglas High School in Florida, told the crowd of two thousand people:

On February 14, I found myself part of a club I never expected to be part of with seventeen other families. I didn't know them beforehand, but I've grown to love them. We don't all agree on everything, but that's fine. We all need each other now, and they have been a very necessary part of our path forward. My wife and I know—and the other families always talk about—how much we hate the fact that we know each other, but we love each other anyway.

South African bishop Desmond Tutu makes clear that there is a strong relationship between pain and intimacy: "We don't really get close to others if our relationship is made up of unending hunky-dory-ness. It is the hard times, the painful times, the sadness and the grief that knit us more closely together."

We don't all share the same degree or type of pain, but we share the vulnerability of loss, of change. We can lie in bed feeling helpless and unseen. We can feel as if we don't count, can "scratch the walls for meaning and hear no echo anywhere," in the words of John O'Donohue. This calls forth compassion.

Compassion doesn't mean we don't fight; it means we find strength in connection and understanding more than we find it anywhere else.

Paco Luagoviña, the Zen Buddhist priest we met in the previous chapter, has been trying to start a substance abuse clinic in New York State, a holistic wellness clinic to deal with the opioid epidemic. "There is an epidemic in the U.S. that is particularly afflicting the middle-class, mostly white community," he says. "These kids are dying of overdoses for a lot of reasons, including that there is no clinic to take care of this particular population. I sit in front of a government group, where there is a supervisor and a council. And I make my pitch about opening up a clinic in their area. And they say, 'Not here. Not in my neighborhood,' even though you're dealing with their own kids. How do you deal with that, you know? How do you bring in your meditation practice?" Paco said he tries to re-center himself by looking at workers in hospice care, people who bear daily witness to other people's deaths day after day, aware of their own emotions but also mindful of whose emotions are center stage. He needs that reminder, he said; otherwise, he will be frozen in sorrow. "Because it breaks my heart. Sometimes I wanna cry. I lost a grandson at the age of twenty-two, twelve years ago, to an overdose. Just a beautiful, beautiful kid. A part of me died when he died. So when I go before these communities, I have to be non-judgmental and really understand their fear, their ignorance. I still hurt. I still cry inside, but it's the only way to deal with it."

SCULPTING THE PAIN

ONCE WE'VE AWAKENED to an issue or cause and we take action, how do we sustain our response over time?

Trauma, disappointment, exhaustion, and overwhelm saturate our emotional lives, our identities, and our beliefs. Not long ago, May Krukiel was a faculty member at the Garrison Institute wellness program in New York, as was I. She pointed out how we might carry and communicate these effects bodily—in our posture, our facial expressions, and our overall body sense. During a program that offered tools of meditation and yoga to domestic violence shelter workers, May led an exercise to explore that somatic phenomenon, which she adapted from a workbook called *Transforming the Pain: A Workbook on Vicarious Traumatization* (New York: Norton, 1996).

In this exercise, people worked in pairs. As May read a script aloud, person A and later person B sculpted their bodies into a posture or position that best expressed their response to the reading. May's script detailed a typical day for people who work at shelters. With a few adaptations, it could easily apply to other stressful and demanding environments.

May read:

The phone rings. It is the district supervisor, saying the budget you submitted had not been approved. You have to find more places to cut, without disrupting essential services. Your assistant suddenly seems depressed and isn't communicative. Your office mate has become belligerent and is too communicative. A crisis has erupted between two residents who are frustrated, stressed, and nearly hopeless. And on a personal note, your health insurance company, having assured you they had all the paperwork they needed to process your claim, writes to tell you they don't have all the paperwork. The doctor's office says they sent it. The company says it never received it. What more can you do?

And on it went.

Participants listened to the vignette, took a moment to settle into their feelings, and then used their bodies to convey their reactions: posture, facial expressions, eyes . . . a full-body response. Once they found the right manifestation of the reaction, they were asked to freeze for a moment or two and allow themselves to really feel their pose.

Time and again, I looked out over a room of people curled over, trying to push away what they were hearing and feeling with arms spread, muscles rigid, and eyes squeezed shut or holding themselves as though they could ward off the pain and keep from fragmenting . . . not breathing and not ready to hear one more thing. It was so honest. So powerful. So sad. I couldn't help but think, *What if we were all walking around this way, as literal representations of how we are hurting or simply so very tired within?* A symbolic exercise maybe, but also very real.

As the exercise of working with vicarious trauma continued, the person who had not molded themselves to the mood brought up in them by the script would look at their knotted-up partner and gently begin to unwind them. Clenched fists were invited to open. Hands that blocked seeing or hearing would instead start signaling an embrace. Between these gentle urgings and self-guided movement, you could see people uncoiling out of that fetal position and standing in a form that was empowered, calm, and whole. Their posture conveyed balance, harmony, groundedness, and dignity.

The newly unfurled person was then asked to form a body memory of this new, open posture and to consider using it in the future whenever strength and hope were needed.

We look at our habitual reactions to pain and consider whether they serve us well anymore, even if they once did. If those reactions are rejecting, denying, or trying to not feel anything so as to soldier through, I'd suggest acting them out in this kind of body sculpture to see if that's the posture you want to maintain in your life. Then, unfurl, open, feel the greater balance in your stance, honor your body's innate knowledge of how to wobble in coming to balance if that's what happens. Breathe deep. Remember resilience just demands we respond in this moment for this moment. It's not the same as a long-term self-improvement plan. Open to what is. Let go of those add-ons we're conditioned to pile on with: don't be afraid of what you are feeling. One way or another, we need to process the tension, either as a torturous experience or something we can open up to.

As Joel Daniels said about being present with pain, "It comes down to my trying to come back to my body. Am I sitting up straight? How am I breathing? Am I breathing shallowly? The more I've done this, the easier it has become to catch myself when I've gone off. No one is always present."

LIFE HAS NOT FORGOTTEN YOU

YOU CAN TAKE one small step toward a different relationship to what is by reaching out to someone or allowing someone to reach out to you. Create—with words or images or food or the way you pay attention to strangers or a new way of relating to your body or those you work with and for. Listen. Take one small step toward the unknown, toward acting without depending on an immediate result, thereby relying on a different sense of meaning. "Hope is not the conviction that something will turn out well," Václav Havel, the Czech dissident, writer, and statesman, said, "but the certainty that it is worth doing no matter how it turns out."

Some things just hurt. And no matter what, we are not alone. Take one small step to allow whatever helping hands are coming toward you to reach you or to extend a helping hand to someone else in some way.

As the Austrian writer Rainer Maria Rilke wrote, "So you must not be frightened . . . if a sadness rises up before you larger than any you have ever seen; if a restiveness, like light and cloud-shadows, passes over your hands and over all you do. You must think that something is happening with you, that life has not forgotten you, that it holds you in its hand; it will not let you fall."

When I'm in some kind of pain, I've found that this can be

one of the worst components of what I experience . . . feeling that I'm all alone, my nose pressed up against the window looking into the space where everyone else has gathered, to enjoy a moment or comfort one another, to be a part of life. I'm somehow excluded, unaccounted for, and no one even notices I'm outside. It's the worst and most habitual add-on I use.

I've been experiencing this since my childhood, when the habit of feeling different and excluded got acculturated, and working with it since college, when in my Asian philosophy class that habitual reaction was challenged upon hearing the Buddha's statement, "There is suffering in life." The subtext was, "It's not just you. You're not weird and different and totally cast aside. You're just hurting."

And I've come to see, even in the worst circumstances, that life has not forgotten me, it has not forgotten us. No matter how despairing or cut off we can feel at any given time, we are not actually severed from the essential flow of life or from one another. If we get quiet for a while and pay careful attention, this is what we realize.

PRACTICE: LOVINGKINDNESS
TOWARD OURSELVES

LOVINGKINDNESS MEDITATION BEGINS with a suggestion to sit comfortably. Sit comfortably physically, sit comfortably emotionally. This isn't a practice where we strive to make something special happen, or seek to fabricate a state, or manufacture anything, but rather we get in touch with a more natural space within us.

You can close your eyes if you feel comfortable; if you are accustomed to meditating with your eyes open, that's fine. And if your eyes are closed and you start to feel really sleepy, it's a good idea to open them, then continue with the practice.

Once your posture is established, begin by actively taking delight in your own goodness. Because so much of our time can be spent remembering the mistakes we've made, our negative actions, that here we consciously point our attention toward something good that we've done. It may be a small thing, but bring it to mind. And if no particular action comes up, think of a good quality that's alive within you. We do this not to be egotistical or conceited but to rejoice in the potential for goodness that we all share in.

We then silently repeat phrases that reflect what we would wish most deeply for ourselves, not just for today but in an enduring way. Phrases that are big enough, that are general enough, so they can represent a gift we would give to ourselves, and also ultimately to others. This is what we would wish for all beings everywhere, beginning with ourselves. The feeling tone is one of generosity or gift-giving, like handing someone a birthday card and saying, "May you have a great year." It's not pleading or even asking. We are offering a quality of attention and care that is different from our usual way of relating to ourselves.

Some of the traditional phrases we use:

"May I live in safety. May I be safe," which relates to everyone's desire for some basic security and protection from harm.

"May I have mental happiness," which refers to peace and joy in our minds.

"May I have physical happiness," which means health and freedom from pain.

"May I live with ease," meaning may the elements of daily life like work and family, relationships, go easily, not be such a struggle.

Pick the ones you want to use and bring them together.

"May I be safe. May I have mental happiness. May I have physical happiness. May I live with ease."

You can use these phrases or any others that are more personally meaningful to you. Just gather all of your attention behind one phrase at a time, as though you were planting a seed in the ground, and then let it go. Keep repeating the phrases. Find a rhythm that's pleasing to you, with enough space and enough silence so the phrases are emerging from your heart.

May I be safe.

May I have mental happiness.

May I have physical happiness.

May I live with ease.

Whenever you find your attention has wandered away from the phrases, gently begin again. No matter where your mind has gone, no matter how far away it has wandered, it doesn't matter. You can actively practice kindness in that moment. Gently let go, gather your energy together, begin again.

"May I be safe. May I have mental happiness. May I have physical happiness. May I live with ease." Or whatever phrases you may be using.

Now visualize yourself sitting in the center of a circle. The circle is made up of the most loving beings you've encountered in this life, or maybe they're people you've never met but who have inspired you in some way. Perhaps they exist in the current time, maybe they've existed historically or even mythically. That's the circle. It's like a circle of love, loving energy. There you are in the center. You can experience what it's like to be the recipient of that quality of attention, of care, as you gently stay in touch and repeat the phrases of lovingkindness for yourself. "May I be safe. May I have mental happiness. May I have physical happiness. May I live with ease."

Many emotions may arise. You may feel joyous, you may feel grateful, you may feel embarrassed, like you'd just like to duck down and have them each offer lovingkindness to one another, forgetting about you. Whatever emotion it is, you can let it come and let it pass as though it were washing through you. The touchstone is the repetition of the phrases. And here, too, whenever you find your attention wandering, it's fine. That is the magic moment of the meditation. We practice letting go; we practice beginning again.

May I be safe.
May I have mental happiness.
May I have physical happiness.
May I live with ease.

To close the session, you can let go of the visualization, dissolve the circle. Keep silently repeating the phrases of lovingkindness for a few more minutes. You're making the offering at the same time you're receiving the energy.

For all the time we usually spend judging ourselves, putting ourselves down, we are recapturing that energy, that force. Let it fill your body. Let it fill your being.

When you feel ready, you can open your eyes. Pay attention to whatever effect the meditation may have had and notice throughout the day whatever quality it may be cultivating.

5

COMING HOME TO OURSELVES

✳

Deep in our hearts, we all long for a feeling of being at home: in this body, in this mind, with someone else, on this planet. Somewhere. If we look carefully at our actions—what we say or do, what we refrain from saying or doing—we can sense within them an urge toward wholeness, toward happiness. This urge to find a home, to find happiness, to make ourselves feel whole again, to build resilience, is a message hidden inside telling us to take care of ourselves. Even if we look at addictions—whether we're entangled with alcohol or drugs, food, gambling, or sex—whether it's a quiet problem or it has blown our lives apart—at the root, we find an urge to feel something unfractured, significant, real.

The basic, universal wish for one's own happiness is ultimately constructive. It's not selfish and it's not wrong, although those who dedicate so much of their time trying to help others often tend to consider such a wish to be too self-centered.

But in truth, this self-nurtured happiness is replete with inner abundance and resourcefulness—the wellspring of energy within that allows us to serve, offer, create. When we are constantly confronted by situations and injustices in the world that we want to change, we can feel guilty that we're never doing enough or feel personally responsible for correcting everything that is at all wrong.

If we don't think we can ever do enough, if we're taught to believe we could never *be* enough, we won't be able to keep on giving. Whatever we do will seem insufficient, and we won't derive much joy from it.

The good news is that there are ways to practice happiness, thereby strengthening ourselves and ultimately strengthening our capacity for service. We used a simple tool for this during the program for domestic violence shelter workers at the Garrison Institute. It illustrates how naturally we all have something we have tried, or have regularly done, to find replenishment or upliftment.

YOUR HABITUAL PATTERNS OF RELIEVING STRESS

TO BEGIN THIS exercise, make three columns on a piece of paper. After reflecting for a while, in the first column, write down your biggest stressor.

In the second column, write down what you do in the face of that stressor to take a break, to build resilience, to make yourself whole.

In the third column, after reflecting on what you wrote in the first two columns, write down how you feel about what's in the second column.

What people wrote in the first column covered a broad range: from the truly traumatic to overwork, to bad communication with colleagues. In the second column, they listed an array of what we generally consider bad habits (excess drinking, drugs, anger, over-eating, etc.) as well as some positive tendencies, such as exercising and getting out in nature. In the final column, we asked people to honestly reflect on their habitual responses to stress and how they sought to feel whole. Maybe they had written down, "I go out into nature," in the second column and then reflected, "Well, it's been about seven years since I did that," or they had written down, "Lots of drinking," and began to reflect on the negative consequences in their lives.

In the same spirit of inquiry, I have long had a habit of asking people I come across what they do to find resilience. The answers are almost always noteworthy. For example, Myles Horton, founder of the Highlander Folk School in Tennessee, whom I mentioned in the previous chapter, simply said, "I look at the mountains."

I love that.

A friend of mine who does housing advocacy work told me, "I think of our bodies as made of stardust." (Which apparently is true, according to a paper by the astrophysicist Karel Schrijver and his wife, pathologist Iris Schrijver, which explains how everything in us originated in cosmic explosions billions of years ago, how our bodies are in a constant state of decay and regeneration, and why Joni Mitchell was right when she wrote the song "Woodstock.")

When Shantel Walker, the fast-food wage activist from chapter 1, is swallowed up by the demands of her struggle, she avoids burning out and taking it out on herself or those around her by getting out and riding a bike. It's not about finding a destination. It's just about the movement, the change of scenery. "Being on the bike takes my mind off things for a while," she says.

Susan Davis, who has worked against poverty for decades, talked to me about certain touchstones that are important for her, including taking time to read and time to meditate in the morning with her wife. "I also find healing and refuge and solace by connecting with trees and leaves," Susan said. "I carry an image in my mind of when the wind is blowing and leaves on the trees are shimmering. Wind is not always with us, and light's not always here, and yet it *is* always here. I can get preoccupied and let monkey mind [i.e., distractedness] take over, but I can bring it back in a second with just that awareness."

People do lots of things to reconnect and recharge: swim, sing, run, dance, gaze at the stars.

What do you do, and how do you feel about it?

If you seek to make change in the world, in whatever way, in whatever scope, and you don't consider this, you may end up— perhaps you will *likely* end up—not taking good enough care of yourself.

Shelly Tygielski, whom we met as a twelve-year-old in chapter 2, is now in her forties, and still an activist. She has been an involved participant in women's marches and worked on local political organizing. As a mindfulness teacher, she has offered classes to the Parkland community in the wake of the shooting at Marjory Stoneman Douglas High School, and she has been involved in creating networks of support for those affected by gun violence.

Shelly wrote an article for *Mindful* magazine on self-care in a politically charged time. In it, she made several key points, including these two:

The need to be prepared for activist burnout. Shelly recommends designing a wellness plan, which some call a *coping bank*. This allows you to accept the fact that activism may take a toll on your body and mind. It's stressful, so be strategic and prepare in advance for the possibility of a bit of a meltdown. Start by taking small, achievable steps, and be practical.

The benefits of building a self-care community. If you have a small network of individuals who will hold you accountable for your self-care plan, it's much more likely to work, since when we get overstressed, the adrenaline rush can cause us to overlook our real condition. These friends will respond when you are in burnout/fatigue/agitated mode and have your back when you say no. They will intervene and help you to get back in touch with your body and mind.

Shelly, among many others, has pointed out that we often neglect self-care out of a (mistaken) belief that attending to it is being selfish. Rev. angel Kyodo williams Sensei is an author, Zen priest, and founder of the Center for Transformative Change, an organization dedicated to bridging the inner and outer lives of social change agents. With her long career in activism and advocacy, Rev. angel clearly distinguishes between self-care and self-indulgence:

> I'm always asking people who are working for social justice, "And what about you? Are you not part of that group

of people who are suffering? And would you permit the people in your life to run themselves into the ground?"

And they respond, "No, of course not. This is what we're working towards."

I say, "Well, if that's what we're practicing is to run ourselves into the ground in order to have justice, at what point will we practice something different? Because whatever we practice is what we *will* practice. If we are practicing running ourselves into the ground for the sake of justice, then that's what we'll continue to practice."

In the same way, one of the residents in the residential community I used to lead was flying through the house and I asked, "What are you doing? Where are you rushing off to?"

She said, "I'm going to yoga."

I simply said, "You're rushing to go relax?" and she stopped.

LACK OF SUPPORT FOR SELF-CARE

UNFORTUNATELY, THE ORGANIZATIONAL cultures we build around change often do not, as Shelly and Rev. angel have pointed out, support self-care. A number of studies have looked at the problem and broken down notable components. Professors Cher Weixia Chen and Paul C. Gorski, from the George Mason University School of Integrative Studies, conducted a study of social justice and human rights activists. The researchers reported an overall lack of attention to burnout within the activist groups they studied. Participants reported guilt and shame associated with considering their own well-being, which they came to think of as *in conflict with* the selflessness of their work. The overwhelming majority of the people studied could not think of a single conversation or mentorship activity concerning self-care, and a number of them described their cultures as hostile to any discussion of symptoms of stress, which one interviewee referred to as a "culture of martyrdom."

Even if a workplace supports self-care, even if you support it for others, you might find that you are leaving yourself out. Rachel Gutter was in the middle of the dream job of her life as the founder of the Center for Green Schools when she started to notice an undercurrent of something just not right. She told me:

> I had so much drive around the opportunities to transform schools into places that put students in touch with nature, and yet I didn't hold enough space for myself. I wasn't living a well-rounded life. More and more, that started to take its toll. I started to see the impact of the inauthenticity that came with being a leader who said all the right things—"I want you to live a three-dimensional life, I want you to take vacations, I want you to get off your screens at night"—while also being a leader who believed work/life balance was for everyone else, didn't take her own vacations, and would send an email at 10:30 p.m., making my employees think they were supposed to respond at 10:32.
>
> When I realized I was becoming less and less equipped to be a good leader for my teams, I was able to give myself permission to spend more time inwardly focused. While helping others, I was able to reclaim what I had lost for myself.

Self-care is not simply about *me* time. It can have a lot to do with a sense of fraternity and sisterhood, because we're actually replenished and nourished by fellowship. It's enlivened by being in community with others, being able to offer something worthwhile to others. I remember watching documentaries about the Freedom Riders of the civil rights movement, who seemed exultant at a life with meaning. I was so inspired to believe that there could be a community built on non-violence, shared values, and love.

There's something very powerful about seeing how any one person connects to the resilience of the human spirit. How we have the opportunity not just to be fighting for change but at the same time to have some joy, a sense of gladness, because obviously, that fight is often not easy.

We can take pleasure in a movie, a story, a good meal shared with a friend, without allowing denial of the pain in the world to sweep us away. We can remind ourselves that we deserve to be pleased, to smile and laugh. There is a lot of suffering out there, to be sure. And there is also valor, and mercy, and one another, and love.

AWAKEN JOY

ADY BARKAN, WHO came down with ALS, posted a series of tweets in March 2019 about a hug he received from his young son Carl:

> "That was the best hug I've ever had," I told him when he was done, trying more than anything to sear it into my mind's eye . . . Because when the daily grind of living a nearly para-lyzed life becomes too much, when I am exhausted and de-pressed and hopeless, I want to return to that hug. I want to

imagine that there are similar hugs in my future . . . That's also the only way, I think, for all of us to persevere through the atrocities and the hate and the lies . . . We have to hold on to the precious beauty, to the moments of triumph, and fight in the hope that there are more victories to come, more beauty and love in our future.

Joy is there. We need to decide to look for it, and as Shelly says, we need to make it a priority in our lives.

To retain our vitality, it's important to be able to switch focus from the negative realities of the world to the positive ones, to regain our capacity for joy, positivity, and connection. From playwright Sarah Jones: "I actually think my work grew from the deepest, most resilient part of me, which was innately playful and happy. And it only began to feel truly satisfying and develop in the thrilling ways I always hoped it would when I did the internal work of connecting with more balance and joy in my life."

Joel Daniels, the storyteller/activist who wrote *A Book About Things I Will Tell My Daughter*, talked with me about finding the power to nourish himself through his relationship with his daughter:

My daughter helps me a lot. She is a very big source of inspiration for me, a constant reminder of what the purest form of love looks like. We're all looking for something because we're human and there's a need to fill that void. Well, that void can be filled with love—self-love. If it's not that healthy kind of love, then you're going to try to find love in other things, in things that are really not consistent, reliable. It comes back to loving yourself because that's going to replenish you.

Many people say these days that society is broken, but as we consider repairing its fractures, we also need to look to see what is not broken. Zainab Salbi—an Iraqi woman who founded Women for Women International to provide support to women survivors of war—tells a story that speaks beautifully to this point. When she returned to the United States from working abroad, Zainab would often talk about a woman she had met in Afghanistan—the travails the woman had suffered, the trauma, the injustice. One day, Zainab was startled to realize that she wasn't also speaking about the fact that the woman was an attorney, had inner resources, had skills. Powerfully, she questioned the completeness of her own compassion if she wasn't quite seeing the woman as the full human being she was.

It's uplifting to see that many changemakers do now include taking care of themselves as a vital part of their mission in the world. They know that truly taking care of themselves—so that they can be of the most value—is indeed something that speaks to a deep part of who they are. It's part of their overall desire to feel a sense of home and belonging. It is *not* a luxury.

If someone seems grim and desperate in their efforts to change the world, I usually bring up the civil rights movement. "People didn't march sobbing," I remind them. "They marched singing." I'm thinking of singing done by people like Bernice Johnson Reagon, the activist who used her powerful alto to spread the message of the Student Nonviolent Coordinating Committee. Reagon, who went on to co-found the a cappella group Sweet Honey in the Rock, was featured in a 1991 film called *The Songs Are Free*. She spoke with journalist Bill Moyers about how something that nurtures the soul can simultaneously be enlisted to effect change:

Sound is a way to extend the territory you can affect. Communal singing is a way of announcing you are here and possessing the territory. When the police or the sheriff would enter mass meetings and start taking pictures and names, and we knew our jobs were on the line, and maybe more . . . inevitably somebody would begin a song. Soon everyone was singing and we had taken back the air in that space.

Jonathan Capehart of *The Washington Post* hosted a podcast series entitled *Voices of the Movement*, exploring how music propelled the civil rights movement in the United States. In the series, Capehart interviewed Ruby Sales, a longtime activist whose involvement dated back to the 1965 Selma-to-Montgomery march. "As a little black child in the South," Sales said, "I could sing 50 songs and that was the way in which I was connected with my elders, with my ancestors. . . . It was our inner selves. It was the essence of who we are as a people. It was a repository of our hopes, the repository of our dreams, the repository of our victories, and the repository of our defeats. . . . Without songs, we couldn't have had a movement. . . . It was where we embodied our courage."

There is plenty to weep about, and it can be good to cry, but by the time we're marching, or deeply listening, or envisioning a brighter day, we are relying on some energy flowing. Our hearts need to be opening, not collapsing under the pressure of hopelessness.

We all are aided by appreciating the good in our lives, the availability of beauty, the uplifting energy of community. We are nourished by being able to connect to something bigger, both in our personal lives and in viewing the world. In Buddhist teaching, it is called *gladdening the mind*, creating an ease of heart that can accompany us in times of adversity or trauma.

Lynn Nottage speaks of love and light and darkness:

I need to circle back to love. I can't dwell too much in the darkness. The darkness for me is not a creative space, but that doesn't mean I don't seek light in dark places. I have found light in the form of human resilience in midst of the protracted war in the Democratic Republic of Congo, or in the Rust Belt, where people persevere despite the lack of prosperity. Or in the struggle of an elephant that's on the verge of being poached, as illustrated in my play *Mlima's Tale*. Like Mlima, for me, it all begins with the things I love.

When (or even before) our work starts to become discouraging and inspiration has dried up, there are practices we can do to build a reservoir of well-being, refreshment, and ease in both our bodies and our minds. Consciously reflecting on what we love, what we have to be grateful for, is one example of such a practice. It's not meant to make us stupidly negligent of real suffering—in fact, it does the opposite. What we have to be grateful for tends to get so little airtime in our consciousness that the buoyancy it can provide to help us look openly and courageously at all of our experience is unavailable to us. With renewed well-being, we are able to see that our path of trying to make a difference may be a long path, and full of obstacles, but it is a good path.

We all tend to have our own means of gladdening the mind.

Friedrike Merck is an artist, an activist, and a philanthropist. She talked to me about the refuge of nature she created as a child and the joy of singing as an adult:

My older sister died when I was seven years old and she was thirteen. I know that the beauty of nature saved me and entertained me, and gave me an endless, astounding fascination for the natural world. I grew up near a swamp. We weren't allowed to have TV. We'd go outside. I was always outside. And I used to be the cheerleader in the family. "Oh, come look at the beautiful sunset. Oh, isn't that a beautiful mountain?"

As an adult, along with her art and delighting in her son, Friedrike came to a greater ease of heart by getting sober, meditating, and singing:

Eighteen years ago, I stopped drinking and began meditating. I sat in meditation for twenty minutes, and I then sat for four years without missing a day. It was really profound. At the same time of becoming sober, I started working with somebody using sound and resonance as a healing tool. It was really enormous, and I started singing again. I think that singing has a spiritual element to it that's deeply visceral and profound and cuts across all spiritual practices, whether it's polytheistic or monotheistic or Buddhist. I joined a choir! And within the choir, I have found a community that has been extraordinary and sincere in its welcoming. I am just so happy.

When we see that appreciating what's good in our lives is right, not wrong, we can feel it lifting us and replenishing us. We need that. It gives us the strength to also look at pain in a different way. If we're looking *only* at pain, we get exhausted. We have to look at pain skillfully, but there's a place for letting the joy emerge in the midst of the pain as well.

Sarah Jones speaks about spreading the joy, what she calls *benevolent contagion*.

I hope that when people listen to a piece of heart-opening music or see a soulful mural on the street, there is a benevolent contagion that helps them create their own art, or have the audacity to dance or skip (literally or otherwise) for a moment on their way to their car, or to listen lovingly and attentively to the inner voice that tells them to try a new recipe or wear the paisley shirt with the striped socks when convention says not to. I know that's how experiencing other people's art affects me. And the same disruption that leads to people protesting in the streets is also connected to any liberation from groupthink that enables people to hear and heed their own drum beat a little better—to even remember it's there.

GENTLE DOSES, EASY STAGES

TO OPEN OUR minds and hearts and stay in touch with the light, we practice gladdening our minds: cultivating generosity, acknowledging joy, seeing what we have to be grateful for. In doing so, we build an inner resource that enables us to persist through anything.

In 1984, IMS brought the renowned Burmese meditation teacher Sayadaw U Pandita to Barre to lead a three-month retreat. My friends Joseph Goldstein and Jack Kornfield and I had never met him before, but we issued the invitation because we had heard that he was a remarkable teacher, and so we committed to practice under his guidance. Once we met him, our experience confirmed what we had heard. We also found that he was very tough, demanding, and even fierce as a teacher.

One day, we were in the meditation hall, and someone asked, "How long should I pay attention to physical pain while meditating before I move my attention to something easier?" (This might include listening to sound, paying attention to a part of the body that doesn't hurt, consciously shifting to something like loving-kindness for yourself and others.) I thought that given Sayadaw U Pandita's usual intensity, he would suggest something like, "You should be with the pain until you fall over."

Instead, he replied, "Don't be with it very long. Pay attention to something easier, then bring your attention back to the pain. Leave it again."

He went on, "It's not wrong to just be with the pain . . . and be with the pain. . . . But you'll likely get exhausted. Why not build in balance all along the way?"

Hearing that, I almost fell over. Surprised as I was, though, I knew him by then as someone who had incredible integrity, so I knew he believed it to be good advice. I thought, *He doesn't pander. He's the furthest thing in the universe from someone who would say something untrue just to be nice or consoling.*

We can extrapolate from that teaching on physical pain what we might need to work effectively with heartache, trauma, or extremely bad circumstances. It points us to a key instruction in trauma therapy: titrate. You can't do it all at once. You can't absorb all that pain at once.

In 2019, when I was hospitalized with a severe infection, I well remember the first time I was able to get out of bed and walk down the hospital corridors using a walker. The physical therapist accompanying me seemed to find me quite amusing. At one point, she said, "It's not a race, you know. You'll get farther if you stop and rest periodically." I started taking that as advice for my life in general.

Sometimes it feels like we have to run a race. We have to beat the onslaught of hatred and divisiveness, the beleaguered planet, the economic and political disenfranchisement. They threaten to rush past us, as though the planetary metabolism were speeding up. But in truth, stopping and resting periodically helps us go farther.

We have our goals and our dreams, where we want to get to, what we want to accomplish and change, but we are, each of us, in a body with its limitations. As we stretch and reach out, we need to, as René Daumal says in his novel of mountain climbing, *Mount Analogue:*

> Keep your eye fixed on the way to the top, but don't forget to look right in front of you. The last step depends on the first. Don't think you've arrived just because you see the summit. Watch your footing, be sure of the next step, but don't let that distract you from the *highest goal.* The first step depends on the last.

Daumal's "first step" reminds me of the upraised heel of Lady Liberty about to take that first step out. We stride, but we also "watch our footing."

There is relief to be found in our lives, like the times discussed earlier that friends have used to awaken joy and care for themselves: riding a bike, walking in nature, giving a hug, getting a hug.

For the sake of our own resilience, we need to strengthen our capacity to accept and absorb joy. If we can't, we *will* get overwhelmed. There's an awful lot of suffering around, and trying to be fully awake to it demands energy, balance, perspective, and the ability to let go of our attachment to immediate results. Ali and Atman Smith and Andrés González, whom we met in chapter 3 and who co-founded the Holistic Life Foundation in Baltimore, say this: "Do the work; don't focus on the results." They work in the harsh environment of under-resourced city schools with kids who know more than anyone should about poverty, drugs, and violence, and yet they remain some of the most cheerful people I know. That cheerfulness is a big part of the gift they give to the schools they work in.

EAT THE BANANA ALREADY

MANY YEARS AGO, I went to spend time with a new friend. He was (and remains) brilliant, loved by many, a committed activist, and someone who taught me a lot in terms of caring for others. At that time and for a considerable time before then, he was also deeply depressed. We walked together along a nearby lake, both in a mode of self-reflection. At one point, he turned to me and said, "You know, I can't even allow myself to enjoy eating a banana."

Assuming causation where there is only correlation is a famous trap in reasoning, but I do think the relationship between his depression and his refusal to allow even the simplest kind of joy into his life was an intricate and intimate one. His awareness of how many people may have suffered to get that banana to be near at hand—underpaid, perhaps far from home, or exploited or frightened—that is real. And that is a sensitivity lost to many of us as we focus narrowly and sometimes exclusively on our own pleasure. I would never want him to lose that sensitivity, and I knew that his awakening greater awareness in people like me was important. I need moral exemplars. I am very influenced by people who say in effect, "I'm not going to eat a banana."

Yet I saw how unhappy he was as he himself brought up the banana, and I know how intense scrupulosity—which psychologists define as a pathological obsession with morality or religiosity—can make us hard and self-righteous, starting with being hard on ourselves. It can leave us feeling incredibly alone.

Sensing his intense sadness, I was tempted to say, "Just eat the damn banana already, would you? Yes, you're inspiring, but what if it kills you? What if you need the potassium?"

That refusal to allow ourselves pleasure and joy is like the Bizarro World version of narcissism. If a narcissistic tendency has us seek attention, power, or status out of a sense of entitlement, this tendency is one of rejection, pushing away vitality or energy or experience rather than endlessly seeking it. Only the terrible bleakness underlying both is the same. It's as if we regard the intense level of suffering we feel in response to others as something sacrosanct, a badge of honor that must not be let go of, or even explored, despite the fact that it may be incapacitating us.

Neuroscientist Richie Davidson has done research on whether meditation can affect our relationship to pain. He was studying physical pain, but since in meditation training we look at physical pain as our template for emotional pain—heartache, disappointment, distress—it is interesting to imagine the applicability of the results extended to our experience of pain generally. What Richie found is that meditators and non-meditators differed most sharply with one another in their experience of what happened before and after the painful stimulus was withdrawn. More of the non-meditators flipped into a cycle of rumination and anticipation—*When is it coming back? How bad will it be?*—while more of the meditators could let it go. Letting it go implies moments of respite, periods of relaxation and peace, rather than seemingly unremitting suffering.

When Richie opened his center at the University of Wisconsin–Madison, the Center for Investigating Healthy Minds (as it was then called), I was on a panel with him as well as the Dalai Lama, John Dunne (a Buddhist scholar from Emory University, now at Richie's center), Barbara Fredrickson (the positive psychology researcher), and Matthieu Ricard. Matthieu is a monk in the Tibetan Buddhist tradition. Before he was ordained, he was a scientist who earned a doctorate in molecular genetics at the Pasteur Institute, and so he is a valuable collaborator in meditation research since he knows both the contemplative world and the scientific world so well. And indeed, he was one of the people involved in the meditation and pain study.

The Dalai Lama was emphatic that the pain should be applied suddenly in the study, which indeed it was; participants did not know whether they were going to get pain or not, nor did they know when the pain might come. It came upon them suddenly, without advance warning. When the Dalai Lama said *suddenly,* I recall that he lurched forward and imitated an abrupt and unexpected jab. At that, Matthieu, sitting next to me, just about leaped into the air. Since so many research projects had begun with refining the interventions by starting with Matthieu, I imagine he assumed he'd be soon subject to abrupt and unexpected jabs.

I saw the point His Holiness was making. Physical or emotional pain is often irregular, abrupt, and fitful, and that's what makes it harder to bear. If we always knew when it was coming, we might more easily acclimate ourselves to it. The fact that it comes upon us suddenly is yet another reason to have long-term strategies for working with pain. Hoping it will never come is not a strategy.

EMPATHY, COMPASSION, AND FATIGUE

THE NEUROSCIENTIST TANIA Singer (along with co-author Olga Klimecki) writes, "In contrast to empathy, compassion does not mean sharing the suffering of the other: rather, it is characterized by feelings of warmth, concern and care for the other, as well as a strong motivation to improve the other's wellbeing. Compassion is feeling for and not feeling with the other."

Empathy seems an essential ability in today's world, which can seem awfully cold, even cruel, if people feel they must disdain others and go it alone. On the other hand, when I consider the exhausted, worn-down activists I've met, the international humanitarian aid workers or nurses or parents, they often seem to me to have *plenty* of empathy. So I've come to believe that something else is leading to burnout.

One description of compassion in Buddhist psychology is: "The quivering or trembling of the heart in response to seeing pain or suffering. It is a movement of the heart, a movement toward, to see if we can be of help."

The first part, the quivering, is the *empathy* part. The second part, the movement toward, to see if we can be of help, is the *compassion* part.

While empathy is essential, if we over-identify with the person or people hurting, the empathy turns into empathic distress, where our own discomfort ironically takes center stage. We collapse or run away.

I see the process in sequential terms. The empathy is a *necessary* but not *sufficient* condition for compassion to arise. We feel the empathy, but maybe we're frightened by what we see, and so we crumble. Or we're exhausted, disheartened, overwhelmed: we don't have the energy to move toward. Or we are caught up in blame. I recently met a therapist who found himself mentally blaming his clients, thinking, *I gave you perfectly good advice six months ago. If you'd only listened!*

It's also possible to develop a savior complex—we don't merely go toward, taking that first tentative stride; we go right into the fires of suffering, determined to control them up to the point where we find we ourselves are burning up.

That's why researchers and Buddhist scholars who define compassion rather precisely see it as the solution and prefer, as I do, the phrase *empathy fatigue* to what is conventionally called *compassion fatigue*.

Compassion implies boundaries (movement toward, not into); balance (compassion for all, including ourselves); stability rather than shakiness; and clarity rather than overidentification. Compassion can be cultivated, through practice, and as it develops further, it helps us avoid burnout and fatigue by teaching us how to say no when we need to, without guilt, and learning to build boundaries. You come to know that saying no is a courageous act and can be empowering. It's also empowering for others, seeing you healthy and able to pick things up another day, rather than barreling ahead distressed and harried.

Deep compassion is suffused with equanimity. Compassionate action is then imbued with wisdom—realizing what we can do, what we can't do, and what we cannot control. Over the long run, that clarity will build resilience, the ability to bounce back when we have stepped beyond our limits, exhausted and without the capacity to offer real help.

END Fund CEO Ellen Agler, author of *Under the Big Tree: Extraordinary Stories from the Movement to End Neglected Tropical Diseases*, talked with me about the intersection of empathy and compassion:

I've come to really appreciate the distinction between compassion and empathy. That has helped me a lot. I took great interest in the research that shows that when you're in an FMRI [functional magnetic resonance imaging] machine and you're feeling empathy for someone who is suffering, the parts of your brain that light up are the ones that light up when *you* are suffering. It's almost like you're going through that same kind of suffering. I have definitely seen that lead to burnout. It's a fatigue, and it has affected so many people I've known in the social sector. They can't stay in it for very long because it is exhausting or depressing or they just work too hard until they can't work anymore. So many non-profits are understaffed and under-resourced compared to the enormous aims of their work. You can work 24-7 and still feel like you haven't done nearly enough to address the suffering caused by injustices you are focused on ameliorating.

By contrast, it seems, with compassion you learn to be present for and hold with spaciousness and dignity the pain and suffering of others, without fully absorbing it as your own. You can hold this with an open hand and an open heart and respond and serve in the ways that are possible. But it's important to practice self-care in the midst of it all so you can keep showing up again and again and again. I continue to try to learn that it's more powerful to give from overflow than to give from a place of depletion. For me, it's compassion, more than empathy, that is one of the most critical tools.

AN ILL-FITTING SUIT

AS WE WORK for change, we will be nourished if we can keep in touch with our authenticity, instead of trying to fit into an over-idealized mold of a perfect person. Or worse, a savior. There is a story I first heard from spiritual teacher Ram Dass that I've encountered various versions of over many years. I find it a wonderful description of our daily efforts to conform to the expectations of others, the stories they project onto us, our own assumptions of what perfection must look like, and where it can be found. Here's the story:

A man wanted to have a suit made. So he went to a tailor in town named Zumbach. Zumbach took his measurements and ordered very fine material. After a while, the man went in for a fitting and put on the suit. One sleeve was two inches longer than the other. He said, "Zumbach, I don't want to complain. It's a beautiful suit. But this sleeve is two inches longer than that sleeve."

Zumbach looked affronted. He said, "There's nothing wrong with the suit. It's the way you are standing." And he pushed one of the man's shoulders down and the other one up and said, "See, if you stand like that, it fits perfectly."

The fellow looked in the mirror again, and now there was all this loose material behind the collar. He said, "Zumbach, what's all this material sticking out?"

Perturbed, Zumbach said, "There is nothing wrong with that suit! It's the way you are standing." And he pushed in the man's chin and made him hunch his shoulders. "See, it's perfect."

But with his shoulders all hunched up, there was another problem. "Now my whole rear end is sticking out!" the man complained.

"No problem," Zumbach returned. "Just lift up your rear end so it fits under the jacket." Again the customer complied, which left his body in a completely contorted posture.

"But standing like this the pants are too short."

Zumbach answered, "There is nothing wrong with the suit! If you'll just bend your knees a bit, you'll see the trousers are just right." The customer tried it, and lo and behold, with his knees bent, his rear end lifted, his shoulders hunched, and one shoulder pushing up and the other pushing down, the suit fit perfectly.

The man paid the tailor and walked out of the shop in a terribly awkward posture, with his shoulders lopsided and his head straining forward, struggling to keep all parts of the suit in their right places. He was walking to the bus, and somebody came up to him and said, "What a beautiful suit! I bet Zumbach the tailor made it."

The man asked, "How did you know?"

"Because only a tailor of Zumbach's skill could make a suit fit so perfectly on somebody with as many physical problems as you have."

I think of the moments we take off the suit we have often struggled to conform to: the perfect image, the invulnerable warrior, the giver who never needs to receive. Whatever the story that has been overlaid on us might be, it is something we have taken to heart and embodied. Part of self-care is actually knowing who we are, what we want, where our boundaries are, and being able to genuinely be ourselves instead of contorting and then highly praising whoever has molded our increased pain.

With an ability to let go of the burden of those external dictates, we can stretch, we can relax, we can contemplate different approaches to our roles, our responsibilities, our tailor, and our wardrobe. Sometimes this looks like going on a retreat or a period of silence, a social media withdrawal, or a time of solitude. At other times, it is the introduction of greater simplicity right in the midst of our everyday lives. Can we let go, for example, of an activity that just seems to promote distraction or division?

Can we admit a preference, be amused by our eccentricity, be tender toward our frailty and exultant at our breathtaking ability to keep growing and learning? Can we fight hard for the decent treatment of farmworkers, and remember that we, too, are just human beings, and that there is likely to be the occasional banana?

PRACTICE: CULTIVATING JOY

IN ORDER TO have the resiliency to face difficulties—for example, a friend or client who can't be helped or a day full of sudden changes outside of our control—we need to find and nurture the positive parts of ourselves and make a point of paying attention to experiences that give us pleasure.

Too often, we focus pretty much only on what's wrong with us, or on negative, unpleasant experiences. We need to make a conscious effort to include the positive. This doesn't have to be a phony effort or one that denies real problems. We just want to pay attention to aspects of our day we usually overlook or ignore. If we stop to notice moments of pleasure—a flower poking up through the sidewalk, a puppy experiencing snow for the first time, a kind interchange between strangers—we have a resource for more joy. This capacity to notice the positive might be somewhat untrained, but that's okay. We practice meditation for just this kind of training.

For this meditation, sit or lie down on the floor in a relaxed, comfortable posture. Your eyes can be open or closed.

Now bring to mind a pleasurable experience you had recently, one that carries a positive emotion, such as happiness, joy, comfort, contentment, or gratitude. Maybe it was a wonderful meal or a reviving cup of coffee or time spent with your kids. Perhaps there's something in your life you feel especially grateful for—a friend who is always there for you, a pet excited to see you, a gorgeous sunset, a moment of quiet. If you can't think of a positive experience, be aware of giving yourself the gift of time to do this practice now.

Take a moment to cherish whatever image comes to mind with the recollection of the pleasurable experience. See what it feels like to sit with this recollection. Where in your body do you feel sensations arising? What are they? How do they change? Focus your attention on the part of your body where those sensations are the strongest. Stay with the awareness of your bodily sensations and your relationship to them, opening up to them and accepting them.

Now notice what emotions come up as you bring this experience to mind. You may feel moments of excitement, moments of hope, moments of fear, moments of wanting more. Just watch these emotions rise and pass away. All of these states are changing and shifting.

Perhaps you feel some uneasiness about letting yourself feel too good, because you fear bad luck might follow. Perhaps you feel some guilt about not deserving to feel this happiness. In such moments, practice inviting in the feelings of joy or delight, and allowing yourself to make space for them. Acknowledge and fully experience such emotions.

Notice what thoughts may be present as you bring to mind the positive. Do you have a sense of being less confined or less stuck in habits? Or perhaps you find yourself falling back into thoughts about what went wrong in your day, what disappointed you—these thoughts can be more comfortable because they are so familiar. If so, take note of this. Do you tell yourself, *I don't deserve this pleasure until I give up my bad habits,* or *I must find a way to make this last forever?* Try to become aware of such add-on thoughts and see if you can let them go and simply be with the feeling of the moment.

End the meditation by simply sitting and being with the breath. Be with the breath gently, as though you were cradling it. Then when you're ready, you can open your eyes.

Bring this skill of gentle interest, curiosity, and attention to your encounters throughout the day. Notice pleasurable or positive moments, even those that may seem small.

6

INTERCONNECTEDNESS

✳

A FEW YEARS AGO WHEN I was teaching together with
Roshi Joan Halifax at New Mexico's Upaya Zen Center,
at the end of our retreat Roshi Joan mentioned that the center
was doing a fund-raising drive for the homeless. In response,
the roomful of people seemed politely engaged, eager to do good
somewhere.

Then Roshi Joan introduced her co-abbot, Joshin, and mentioned that he was spearheading this drive because his father had

been homeless. The whole room swiveled in unison to look at Joshin. The world stood still. *Of course,* I thought. *Homeless people will always be someone's father, brother, aunt, child.* My own father had lived on the streets at times. Even though these instances were brief intervals between psychiatric hospitalizations—and were not the most traumatic recollections I had of him—they still stung.

If you don't know anyone in that situation, it's so easy to disassociate from the humanity of someone who is homeless and just walk on by, but if someone you love is living on the streets, sooner or later your heart just breaks for them, even if you are furious that they ran away from their safe nursing home, or are drinking, or couldn't manage a job.

By and large, when a homeless person in St. Louis or Seattle or London or Berlin asks us for money, we're looking at someone most of us have declared to be "other" and therefore of no account, someone who got caught in a whirlwind of external circumstances or internal chaos or terrible habit and was squeezed out onto the streets. These are the people most often overlooked by our society, who receive our indirect attention at best. We're looking at someone who exemplifies one of our most pervasive fears: not belonging.

We're seeing, too, the result of society's priorities, policies, and governance. We're seeing the narrative of our civic engagement, or lack thereof. We're seeing someone's mother, or child, or father—and very likely a trail of broken hearts.

SELF AND OTHER AND THE SPARKS OF ACTIVISM

I AM FASCINATED by the question of how we construct our worldview and what components combine to create our sense of self and other. We are born into communities of race, language, ethnicity, state/country/region, gender, religion, and more, so then where do we anchor our perception of belonging? Do we feel at home only when anchored in a specific identity? Has that identity largely been imposed upon us by stories others tell about us, or is it something we ourselves enlist for courage and self-respect?

And how do we hold that sense of identity? Do we hold it as a meaningful yet porous and mutable thing, or does it hold *us*—keeping us rigidly apart, severed from others, believing ourselves disconnected and alone?

These days, identity is often talked about in terms of *intersectionality*, a word I first heard spoken by Mallika Dutt, the human rights activist we met in chapter 3. We were both on the faculty of a program at the Women's Leadership Center at Omega Institute. When Mallika used the word *intersectionality*, I immediately thought, *That must be the same as interconnection.*

To me, *interconnection* conveys what Zen teacher Thich Nhat Hanh calls *interbeing*, or what is sometimes known as *interdependence.* It is the view that everyone relies on everyone else in this universe—our lives all have something to do with one another, and a bigger picture of life. Often we see ourselves as isolated, independent, sealed off from others, and in that separation, we struggle to seize control somehow.

But what is the reality?

The truth is that everyone is interdependent, connected, reliant on one another. A corollary to this understanding is that everyone counts, everyone matters. Taken together, these two aspects of interconnectedness provide a vision of life that sparks efforts to make a difference in this world. As Mallika went on to define intersectionality, however, I came to see that it meant something else, which actually enhanced my understanding of interconnectedness. She expanded upon her definition in an interview I did with her:

Intersectionality began as a legal concept that sought to help people facing multiple and intersecting forms of discrimination find legal redress. The multiplicity of identities a person could have were very poorly understood—particularly where women of color were concerned—and people were losing discrimination cases as a result. The concept of intersectionality fostered the understanding that you could be experiencing discrimination based on race, class, gender, ability—all at the same time.

Over time, the concept expanded to encompass not just intersections of multiple kinds of oppression but also of privilege. We can come to understand how each one of us has intersections within ourselves: parts of our identity may confer privilege while other parts may invite oppression. A white woman might have race privilege but face oppression on the basis of her gender, or she might have class privilege but might have experienced an accident that made her disabled. All of these dynamics play out at the individual level and also at the institutional level. It's not simply about how we treat each other. It's also about how institutions like the criminal justice system have built-in biases toward and against certain identities.

These intersections also depend on the context we find ourselves in. So, for example, as an immigrant woman in the United States, I may experience some forms of discrimination, but as a Hindu, upper-middle-class woman in India, I have enormous amounts of privilege.

As I contemplated intersectionality, it led me to look at identity—and ultimately belonging—through the lens of multiple social categories. In doing so, I also glimpsed the multifaceted lives I experience every day. I thought of the Buddha saying, "Within this fathom-long body lies the entire universe." I look at my life— one made up of both privilege and vulnerabilities, manifold gifts and terrible losses—and I see that my life has encompassed multitudes and that every aspect of my experience has played and continues to play a part in who I know myself to be.

Two years later, when we co-taught again, Mallika introduced intersectionality by saying, "More and more, a consideration of intersectionality leads me to interconnection."

Understanding intersectionality can lead to appreciating interconnection, because the more we see all of the aspects of who we are and all the aspects of who others are, the less we see ourselves or other people as limited to being only one thing or another. The more connected we feel to ourselves in all our dimensions, the more capable we are of recognizing the longings and fears and joys and sorrows of others.

We connect by recognizing ourselves in one another.

Mallika sees intersectionality as "a really powerful tool to get us to appreciate interconnectedness. When we understand all the ways we are in relationship with ourselves and with one another, we come to see that everything we do affects more than just us. We are in a dynamic interconnected relationship with each other. If we can get to understanding ourselves in that way, what might we imagine for how we can live on this planet together?"

Atman Smith, from the Holistic Life Foundation (HLF), works with schoolchildren using yoga, mindfulness, exposure to nature, and other tools in his hometown of Baltimore. Once HLF gives the kids tools to care for and value themselves, Atman says, inevitably they begin to care for and value others.

You can't ask a kid, or anyone who doesn't love themselves yet, to care about somebody sitting next to them, or somebody halfway across the world, or their community, or the planet, or anything, because they're in a hopeless, angry situation, where they're not connected to anything. It's beautiful to see, though, that once they connect to themselves, a light bulb goes off, like, "Oh, okay. There is something more to this." And they start to see themselves in other people, and they start to care more, and they start to do more, and it just changes them from the core. And it starts to ripple out. They start to care about themselves, and their families, and their friends, and their neighborhood, and everything all together on a bigger scale.

DO WE EVEN SEE EACH OTHER?

THE CLEVELAND CLINIC is well known for its high level of patient care and the core value of empathic action in the clinic's culture. A very effective video from the Cleveland Clinic, created for both patients and practitioners, is called "Empathy: The Human Connection to Patient Care." It begins with a quotation from Henry David Thoreau: "Could a greater miracle take place than for us to look through each other's eyes for an instant?"

Then without any dialogue the camera follows people moving through a hospital, with text appearing that simply portrays their situation:

Fears he's waited too long.

Tumor was benign.

Tumor was malignant.

They saw . . . something . . . on her mammogram.

He's worried about how he is going to pay for this.

Too shocked to comprehend treatment options.

Wife's surgery went well.

As we watch, these people come together on an elevator, pass each other on adjacent up and down escalators, and sit together in waiting rooms.

The video closes with this question:

If you could stand in someone else's shoes, hear what they hear, see what they see, feel what they feel, would you treat them differently?

That hits home. The hospital setting reveals humanity in so many of our stages of delight and grief and worry and love. So does every street corner, and airport, and classroom, and home.

How is it, then, that the people we encounter in an ordinary day can seem so far away, so remote from our field of concern? How is it that we might witness a mother who can't afford mental health treatment for her child, or an overwhelmed adult caring for their aging parent, or a young person struggling to find a job . . . and not resonate with their experience?

Pedro Noguera, a Distinguished Professor of Education at UCLA, focuses on the ways schools are influenced by social and economic conditions. He's especially articulate about our culture of disconnection:

We live in a society that allows mentally ill people to live on the streets. We incarcerate so many people in America and people accept it as normal. There are so many conditions that are really just, to me, atrocities that we accept.

The question is, what do you do to address it?

Some colleagues have called it the "Crisis of Connection." It's all about the need to address the empathy gap, the inability people have to identify with the suffering of others, when those others are from a different group, different race, different nationality, different culture, religion, et cetera. I do think that's where we're at. I think the way to counter that empathy gap is through education. Finding ways to appeal to people's sense of humanity is essential.

In a similar spirit, Arian Moayed co-founded Waterwell, a civic-minded theater company that uses entertainment and arts education to inspire audiences and students to change their lives and the world in which they live. Arian speaks about the power art can have to bring people in closer connection:

I believe that if art is done purposefully, we can actually change people's lives one by one, and that kind of change can affect a myriad of people. Deep down, how do you teach that? How do you tell people to be a better citizen, to be better in society? There are so many tools, but one of the things that Waterwell has figured out is something we call the Three E's: excellence, engagement, and empathy.

That is what it is to be on Earth, in a weird way. You want to engage with all of your people. You want to engage one by one with your family and your friends and your kids. You want to always strive to be excellent. You always want to try to see if you can do the best you can, through hard work and love. And empathy is about trying to find a way to understand what it means to not be you and see what else is on the other side.

WHAT WE LEARN FROM LOOKING AT A TREE

THERE ARE MANY avenues that can lead to an appreciation of interconnectedness. Accepting it logically is one thing. Through contemplative practice, we may apprehend it at a more visceral level. If we pay careful attention, we see that phenomena in the natural world, moments of experience, people, and creatures continuously affect one another. Consider the different ways we can view a tree. We can see the tree as a distinctly defined object, a single solitary entity standing there just by itself. We can also look at that tree and sense it as the manifestation of an extremely subtle net of relationships.

The tree is affected by the rain that falls upon it and everything that affects the quality of that rain. It is affected by the wind that moves through and around it and the soil that nourishes it and sustains it. It is affected by the weather and by the sunlight and by the moonlight and by the quality of the air. Its root system can connect it to an ecosystem of underground life for miles around. We can look at the tree and see it is a network of influences and interactions converging. Similarly, we can look at this precise moment in our lives and see it is just the same. We can look at who we are and see it is just the same. Not solitary and isolated but rather connected and interdependent.

This is the truth of our existence: because we live in an interconnected universe, everything is contingent, intertwined, interrelated.

As Thich Nhat Hanh says:

If you are a poet, you will see clearly that there is a cloud floating in this sheet of paper. Without a cloud, there will be no rain; without rain, the trees cannot grow: and without trees, we cannot make paper. The cloud is essential for the paper to exist. If the cloud is not here, the sheet of paper cannot be here either. So we can say that the cloud and the paper inter-are.

"Interbeing" is a word that is not in the dictionary yet, but if we combine the prefix "inter" with the verb "to be," we have a new verb, "inter-be." Without a cloud, we cannot have paper, so we can say that the cloud and the sheet of paper inter-are.

If we look into this sheet of paper even more deeply, we can see the sunshine in it. If the sunshine is not there, the forest cannot grow. In fact nothing can grow. Even we cannot grow without sunshine. And so, we know that the sunshine is also in this sheet of paper. The paper and the sunshine inter-are. And if we continue to look we can see the logger who cut the tree and brought it to the mill to be transformed into paper. And we see the wheat. We know that the logger cannot exist without his daily bread, and therefore the wheat that became his bread is also in this sheet of paper.

And the logger's father and mother are in it too. When we look in this way we see that without all of these things, this sheet of paper cannot exist.

In day-to-day life, a deeper understanding of interconnectedness translates as an ability to perceive the patterns and networks of which we are all actually a part, and it makes clear the fallacy of separation—of self and other.

This clarity of perception is the root of understanding each other.

It's also the root of compassionate action.

TEAMWORK

INTERCONNECTEDNESS ASKS US to let go of rigid differences, to be responsive to the needs of others, to know that taking care of others is an inextricable part of truly taking care of ourselves. As Mallika says in describing her mission, "I have come to understand that my personal happiness and freedom is connected with the well-being of all communities, all species and indeed, all of Earth. It is from this place of interconnectedness that I seek to align purpose, people, and planet."

One of my favorite questions to ask when teaching in a workplace is: "How many people need to be doing their jobs well in order for you to be able to do your job well?"

George Mumford believes that if you come to understand how essential other people are to what you do, you will appreciate how teamwork is necessary in all of life. George, author of *The Mindful Athlete,* is a longtime mindfulness teacher who has worked with athletes at all levels, including the National Basketball Association (NBA). One of his points of focus is what makes us perform less well, particularly under pressure. George points out that when athletes are growing up and playing on asphalt courts and sandlot ball fields, there's a lot of emphasis on individual greatness. And yet, he says, in the end,

It's always better together. The whole is greater than the sum of the individual parts. This idea has to come from love; it has to come from openness. We are social creatures and yes, we are better together than we are out on our own.

In my years working with basketball coach Phil Jackson and his teams, we used to quote Rudyard Kipling's novel *The Jungle Book,* where it says the strength of the pack is in the wolf and the strength of the wolf is in the pack. I refer to that as the dynamic tension between the *me* and the *we:* How can I be myself and at the same time part of something greater than myself?

The only way that's going to happen is through a shared worthy cause and shared values. We all have to value differences, we have to value love and respect, we have to value that each one has a voice and has to be able to express themselves, even if we have to draw out some of the voices of people not so keen on expressing themselves.

We need to figure out how to engage with each other in orderly ways, like the talking stick of the Native American traditions, so we're not all just talking at once. We need generosity, compassion, and appreciative joy: we need to be able to share in others' achievements to enjoy their well-being and happiness. We need a teamwork of the body, mind, and heart, or spirit—being able to be yourself while you allow others to be themselves. It helps when we can keep in mind that people are "just like me": this person wants to be happy *just like me;* this person wants to be happy *just like me;* this person experiences frustration *just like me;* this person makes mistakes *just like me;* this person is not perfect *just like me.*

ISOLATION, LONELINESS, AND MEDITATION

UNFORTUNATELY, THE CULTURE of togetherness and mutual appreciation for each other that George talks about is becoming harder to find. Many people have commented on the decline in our social networks: our circles of friends, our trusted companions, and our churches, clubs, social groups, and bowling leagues—the ways we find to be together. On top of that, we are in an era when people are reporting themselves to be increasingly lonely, experiencing such intense feelings of isolation that it affects their mental and physical health.

Loneliness is not about actual social isolation (the frequency of our contacts with friends and relatives, which as I just noted is itself in decline) or with solitude (choosing to be alone). Loneliness is *perceived* social isolation, feeling that you don't have the level of social contact you would like. When this perception is prolonged, it can become a serious health problem and may even decrease life expectancy.

A 2014 article in the journal *Social and Personality Psychology Compass* described how researchers used data from the Chicago Health, Aging, and Social Relation Study (CHASRS) to test the hypothesis that the effect of loneliness accumulates to produce greater increases in systolic blood pressure than experienced by less lonely individuals. They described how independent of factors like age, gender, ethnicity, medications, or health conditions, higher initial levels of loneliness were associated with greater increases in systolic blood pressure over a four-year period.

And the opposite also appears to be true: that feeling connected and being more connected improves our health. A study published in 2006 in the *Journal of Aging Life Care* showed that increasing the size of a social network for older men over a ten-year period showed a reduction of 29 percent in mortality risk per year.

Sadly, we do not, in general, appear to be moving in that healthier direction. In 2018, a survey by the global health service company Cigna revealed that nearly half of Americans report sometimes or always feeling lonely. Surprisingly, younger people and students report greater levels of loneliness than retirees. One in five people reported that they "rarely feel close to others" and only about half reported having "meaningful, in-person social interactions." According to the Cigna study, loneliness affects men and women and people of different ethnic backgrounds equally. A large number of us are feeling disconnected and alone.

In fact, Vivek Murthy, the U.S. surgeon general during the Obama administration, called loneliness "an epidemic," comparing its impact on health to obesity or smoking fifteen cigarettes per day. A survey by the Kaiser Family Foundation, in partnership with *The Economist* reported that:

More than a fifth of adults in the United States (22 percent) and the United Kingdom (23 percent) as well as one in ten adults (9 percent) in Japan say they often or always feel lonely, feel that they lack companionship, feel left out, or feel isolated from others, and many of them say their loneliness has had a negative impact on various aspects of their life.

The British government was concerned enough about widespread social isolation to appoint a minister for loneliness. We know in our hearts that we are connected, and yet so many of us feel utterly disconnected. Mindfulness may help with that.

Dr. Dilip Jeste, a professor of psychiatry and neuroscience with the University of California–San Diego, says that "spirituality and empathy help a person feel more connected with others. You know you are part of a much larger cosmos. You are never alone. There is something else besides you that will always be there." He also notes that "those who self-reflect have a greater understanding of why they feel lonely."

Many studies bear this out, finding that people who have qualities of wisdom—empathy, compassion, self-reflection—are much less likely to feel lonely. All of these qualities are increasingly being recognized as benefits directly derived from mindfulness and mindful meditation practices. Perhaps a closer look at these practices could make a significant impact on the loneliness epidemic. Ironically, spending quality time by ourselves may help us undo the perception that we are all alone. Meditation, which helps us to glimpse interbeing, can reveal to us that the belief that we're desperately alone is simply mistaken.

HOW EASILY WE JUDGE OTHERS

RESEARCH SHOWS THAT most of us make split-second judgments about people based on superficial differences. We ourselves—and many of the people we care about—may have been the recipients of those judgments. As Sharon Begley, the senior science writer for the online journal *STAT,* wrote in the October 2016 issue of *Mindful* magazine:

> We instantly classify a face by sex, race, age, social status, and emotion, the strongest categories available to the brain. (Evolution sculpted the brain to be attuned to signals that might alert us to possible threats.) Next, the brain immediately and unconsciously activates everything it knows (or believes) about people belonging to the categories—that's how stereotypes are born. In less than a second (hence the name "split-second social perception," as this process is called), those stereotypes act back on our visual system.

She cites the work of NYU psychologist Jonathan Freeman, whose research reveals that as a result of "the baggage we bring to the table," what we literally see is not a straightforward readout of facial features but rather a complex construct with input from the brain's belief system. If we are raised in a cultural context from which we absorb the implicit associations that create bias, the bias will show up, not as conclusions or afterthoughts but as part of our basic way of perceiving the world.

Rachel Gutter, the founder of the Center for Green Schools, whom we met in chapter 4 and who went on to lead the healthy building movement at the International WELL Building Institute, talks about her own experience:

> I remember my boss saying to me, "Gutter, I really need your help building a team that has more diversity on it." And I said, "I'm an Asian Jewish lesbian. Like, what else do you really want?" There's a lot of otherness in me. I grew up as the only Jewish kid in my class. I'm mixed race, short, and was, generally speaking, twenty to thirty years younger on average than the people who I was interfacing with during my time at the Green Building Council. My boss didn't seem to notice my otherness, but I encountered a surprising amount of discrimination and adversity and unconscious bias in my professional community.

Anurag Gupta, in a similar way, faced multiple levels of othering:

> I didn't really understand the concept of race until I moved to the U.S. when I was ten years old. People would constantly ask me a question like, "What are you, or who are you?" I would say, "I'm Anu," but this did not suffice. "No, you're not black, you're not white, and you're not Asian," they would say, always wanting to fit me into their boxes.
>
> I had a pretty strong interest in science from a young age, and I knew that, from a scientific perspective, we're all *Homo sapiens*. Color is just one of the hundreds and millions of things that make us who we are as individuals. Despite what I knew to be true, on an emotional level being confronted with this question of what I was always made

me feel separate, other than, different from those who were around me—and less-than.

This tendency to regard people as "other"—as categorically different from ourselves—extends also to places and things: they are not ours; they are alien to us. As we noted above, this kind of bias is an evolutionary trait, part of our survival wiring. Biases—snap judgments—are what supported early humans in assessing the relative safety or danger of strangers. It's the mechanism we developed to help us decide who or what is a threat. It's a natural habit.

Both research and common sense underscore that when we are afraid of losing a sense of our own identity, snap judgments can transform into ingrained prejudice and antipathy. This dynamic is at work on every level, from spats with friends and loved ones, to neighborhood disputes, to geopolitical conflict. A student of mine recently told me about going to her partner's family's house for Christmas and how she found celebrating a different holiday and spending time with his family to be mildly traumatic, simply because of the difference. "His family was *so* different from my own," she said. "I felt so judgmental of them, but also insecure." This kind of "us versus them" tribal dynamic is going on all around us and often within us. Overcoming it is a matter of first noticing it arise and interrogating whether separation from the "other" actually makes us feel safer.

CONTRACTION AND EXPANSION

AT ONE POINT, meditator and research psychiatrist Jud Brewer, M.D., Ph.D., wrote me an email about his growing awareness of the relationship between his personal meditation practice and his lab's research into habit formation and behavior change. We had been corresponding about what seemed to be the worldwide rise of antagonism toward immigrants and the related sense of divisiveness toward others when he sent this thoughtful response:

I feel like there's an even stronger need to transform this communal energy from hate to love, from separation to connection. This morning it arose that this may be where my personal practice comes together with my lab's research: exploring the experience of contraction vs. expansion and how that manifests in the world in so many ways.

When I heard Jud refer to *contraction vs. expansion,* I thought that he had landed on an evocative metaphor to describe us versus them: *contraction* struck me as the feeling we create for ourselves when we're threatened or afraid. We contract, we close in, we seek separateness, we create rigid boundaries. *Expansion,* by contrast, must mean something like lovingkindness—a more spacious feeling of love, joy, and generosity.

"I like that metaphor," I told him in my reply.

"It's literal," he wrote. Surprised by that response, I suggested we have a longer conversation.

Jud began by telling me about research he started pursuing around 2008: his lab sought to characterize the brains of novice meditators in comparison to experienced meditators using functional magnetic resonance imaging (fMRI) scanners.

Jud and his co-researchers looked at a brain region called the *posterior cingulate cortex* (PCC), which was most active among novice meditators. "When they were feeling guilty, they activated it," Jud said. "When they were craving a bunch of different substances, they activated it. When they were ruminating, they activated it. When they were anxious, they activated it."

What Jud and his team found was that this more active PCC correlated with contraction. "The experience of anxiety, of guilt, of craving, of rumination, all of these," he said, "literally share an experiential component of contraction. We contract when we're afraid. We contract when we're feeling guilty."

By contrast, he explained, when we are able to dissolve our sense of clinging to a rigid, isolating "self" and a corresponding "other" activity decreases in the PCC, with a parallel sense of expansion.

HOW DO WE CHANGE?

BUDDHIST PSYCHOLOGY POSITS that if we respect interconnection, it opens us to the possibility of an unforced altruism that is the natural outcome of how we see the world. As you see life more accurately, you just find you are different from how you were before: less afraid, feeling less alone.

At first, we may be livid when we read the news and detest the people we're reading about. But we come to see that regarding others—ranging from personal acquaintances to government officials—as totally disconnected from ourselves, doesn't help. As I learned from Jud, it activates the part of our brain associated with anxiety, guilt, fear, and rumination. We contract, close up, turn in, turn away. When I am awash in those feelings, I find it hard to keep going or to put effort into taking action. I don't derive strength of purpose or staying power from these contracted states, these times when I can hardly breathe, so caught up in anxiety, guilt, fear, and rumination. If I want to reach out to others, I need to tap into my sense of interconnection, to expand rather than contract.

Expanding and opening to our interconnected reality does not imply that we dissolve all discernment and collapse into gray blobs, tossed about by the world, as some people imagine. It doesn't mean that when we see injustice, we lose the imperative to fight to make things different in the world, to make them better as we see it. We do fight, and maybe even harder than we could before we developed a greater sense of interconnection, but we are sustained by a vision of life that is not based on contraction and estrangement. We do not need to demonize others in order to counteract misdeeds, harm, and injustice. We can work toward change empowered by a sense of expansiveness, interconnection, and compassion. Dr. Martin Luther King Jr. echoed the Buddha, who lived 2,500 years before he did, when he said, "Darkness cannot drive out darkness; only light can do that. Hate cannot drive out hate; only love can do that."

When I look at the often heavy consequences of separation and contraction—dehumanization, cruelty toward creatures, a culture of death instead of life—I feel ever more committed to disempowering disconnection, in every way, in every direction.

To recognize connection doesn't mean we like every single person or approve of their actions or hope they win and accrue more power. It means we're not driven by "us and them" constructs to a point where we're out of touch with a fundamental truth of our lives: we are already connected. We share this planet; we share this life. To recognize our interconnection isn't the same thing as ceding power over our fate to someone else. Regardless of interconnection, we need to engage our inquiring minds and take a close look at power dynamics in whatever situation we find ourselves in.

I might, for example, develop compassion for someone but not want them to be legislating policies that affect my health care choices, the disposition of crime and punishment, the cleanliness of the food I buy, or whether the children in my neighborhood get lunch at school. Maybe I want them in charge of nothing at all, really.

I might develop compassion for someone but also realize that they are not the right person for a particular job or to run an organization I'm involved in. When I have to tell them no, they may be hurt, and I can feel compassion for that pain and soothe it as best I can, but an understanding of interconnection helps me to see that hiring them for the job may create greater pain for them and for others.

I might develop compassion for someone but also reject their efforts to dictate what I do with my life, to exert a power over me that is not healthy for either me or them. I listen to advice with an open ear and heart but I am mindful of the need to take care of myself and maintain the agency we talked about in chapter 2.

And none of this is to imply that moving from contraction to expansion, that developing compassion based on a deep understanding of interconnection, is easy. To be glib or abstract about such transformations would dishonor the tremendous effort people put forward to serve from a place of love instead of hatred. I know it's hard, especially if we're looking at situations of intense suffering and perhaps most difficult if we're looking at situations of people's cruelty. Going toward that, opening to that, can seem unbearable, an insurmountable challenge. Disconnecting from it all can seem like the sanest, safest thing to do in the face of great pain. But after a while, that just begins to feel like giving up.

YOU STILL NEED TO TAKE CARE OF YOURSELF

COMPASSION IS NOT divorced from insight and intelligence. For example, it doesn't always mean reconciliation. We can remain apart from someone while still having compassion for them. I can remember when a longtime student of the Dalai Lama asked him, great vessel of love and compassion that he is, if she should go see her mentally ill mother, who had been a danger to her physical well-being in the past and who was now asking to see her. "You should offer your mother a tremendous amount of lov-ingkindness," advised the Dalai Lama, "from a distance. It's not safe to go see her."

In a similar vein, I was quite taken with a tweet by meditation teacher Ethan Nichtern: "We needn't be in a rush to try to over-ride our alliance in the first place with those [who have been] hurt. Question I often get re compassion meditation: Do you have to practice compassion for those who cause serious harm? Eventu-ally, Yes. But perhaps not before you've acted compassionately on behalf of those who've been harmed."

I was also quite taken with climate change activist Tim DeChristopher's idea of forming a "compassion corps" or "com-munity of compassion"—a way to support each other in compas-sion. Tim served twenty-one months of a two-year prison sentence for an act of civil disobedience: making the winning bids on four-teen oil and gas leases in a Bureau of Land Management auction with no intention of purchasing the lands but with the intention of forestalling development of these lands as an act of protest.

Tim and I talked about how our first job after a traumatic incident may be just to survive, or try to heal, not force ourselves to care about the perpetrator. At times like these, Tim posits, fellow members of our "compassion corps" may serve a role that we cannot. As he told me:

It's vital to have compassion for those who are doing something genuinely wrong. If you really love someone who is in that position of shame, it frees them up to have guilt for what they're doing wrong. I see *guilt* as focused on an action—on what we did wrong—whereas *shame* is focused on ourselves, it's tied up with our identity. Shame tells us not simply that we did something wrong but that we are a wrong person. Compassion for a wrongdoer allows them perhaps to let go of the shame and come to simply appreciate that they have done or are doing something wrong.

It's very difficult, though, to extend that compassion when you're the one who has been harmed. That's where a community of compassion is really critical—trusting that in the cases where we have been traumatized by someone, we might not need to beat ourselves up for not having compassion, not being the one who liberates that person from their shame, and trusting that there can be others out there in our community who can step in.

That's the wonderful thing about grace: grace doesn't have to come from the person who was wronged, whereas forgiveness does. Part of being in solidarity with people

who have been hurt and have been traumatized is not join-
ing in the hatred for the person who did this wrong thing.
The more helpful path can actually be offering grace and
compassion to the person who did something wrong, to
liberate the person who was traumatized to just deal with
themselves, and not have to have any responsibility for the
person who did something to them.

I understand what Tim is saying. When people say to me, "I
don't think I can forgive this person who hurt my family so terribly," I think, *I don't know if that's your job at this moment. Right
now, you have the job of grieving, of working with the pain and hurt.
Forgiving is likely a bridge too far, a kind of image of perfectionism and
a forced concept of compassion that you're holding in your mind.*

Tim goes on to say, "Forgiving can be an impossible standard,
particularly when you're the one who has been hurt. Even if you're
still harboring a lot of resentment or hatred in your heart for that
person, just to restrain your hand from vengeance can be critical.
It helps if you can trust that others can be offering grace while
you're just healing yourself. That's what a compassion corps can
do. Compassion becomes a group effort."

FIGHTING, NOT HATING

WHEN I THINK about how Tim brings compassion to bear on his
relationship with wrongs and wrongdoers, it reminds me of a potent
question an audience member posed when I was in a Berkeley,
California, church, sitting on a panel that included a few Tibetan
lamas and several Western meditation teachers. "When I look at

my own behavior," the person began, "I can see that when I am reckless, or hurtful, or insensitive, those actions are born from a place within me that is full of pain. Then I can proceed to seek change from a place of compassion for myself. But when I look at others, especially in the political arena, I see people committing actions that are cruel, speech that is inciting hatred and division. Yet they don't seem like they are suffering. They often seem rather pleased with themselves. What should I do?"

The question was met by a long period of silence. Finally I responded.

"I'm with you," I said. "I have the same issue. Sometimes I look at certain leaders and think, *If you could just fray a bit at the edges, show me a little vulnerability or frailty, it would be so much easier to consider compassion.* But I consider my body and mind and heart to be like a testing ground. If I see that my misaligned actions stem from pain, I find that a pretty good indicator of what is likely truer for others. I also believe in the capacity of ordinary human beings to experience greatness. If someone settles for a life where their strongest, most accessible idea of happiness is hurting someone else, exercising power over others, being disconnected, I find that to be such a violation of what I believe we are capable of that it actually calls forth compassion from me. Compassion doesn't mean we don't *fight*; it means we don't *hate*."

Often we feel, though, that we are being treated badly; often we may, in fact, *be* being treated badly. People may try to force us—intentionally or not—into feeling alone or not wanted, as we looked at in the earliest chapters.

In that regard, I love the words of Dorothy Allison, the author of *Bastard out of Carolina*: "To resist destruction, self-hatred, or lifelong hopelessness, we have to throw off the conditioning of being despised, the fear of becoming the *they* that is talked about so dismissively, to refuse lying myths and easy moralities, to see ourselves as human, flawed, and extraordinary. All of us are extraordinary."

Rachel Chavkin echoed what Dorothy was saying when she gave her 2019 Tony Award acceptance speech for best director of *Hadestown*, a Broadway play based on the Greek myth of Orpheus journeying to the underworld to rescue his fiancée, Eurydice. "My folks raised me with the understanding that life is a team sport," Rachel said. "That's what is at the heart of this show: It's about whether you can keep faith when you are made to feel alone. And it reminds us that that is how power structures try to maintain control: by making you feel like you're walking alone in the darkness, even when your partner is right there at your back."

WHAT DOES LIVING WITH A VISION OF INTERCONNECTION LOOK LIKE?

IT LOOKS LIKE **Mollie Tibbetts's father, Rob.** The man accused in 2018 of killing twenty-year-old Mollie in Iowa was Mexican. When that news was released, it brought on waves of racial hatred and fearmongering, which the grieving family firmly rejected. Rob Tibbetts said the family was "grateful" to those who respected their pleas to not turn his daughter's death into a political confrontation. "Sadly, others have ignored our request," he wrote. "They have instead chosen to callously distort and corrupt Mollie's tragic death to advance a cause she vehemently opposed."

To the Hispanic community, he added: "My family stands with you and offers its heartfelt apology. That you've been beset by the circumstances of Mollie's death is wrong. We treasure the contribution you bring to the American tapestry in all its color and melody."

At her funeral, he said, "The Hispanic community are Iowans," revealing that many of them had embraced him as he searched for his daughter in recent weeks. "They have the same values as Iowans. As far as I'm concerned, they're Iowans with better food."

It looks like Mallika's inspiration to see in intersectionality the evidence of interconnectedness and her aspiration to "align purpose, people, and planet."

It looks like Joshin working with homeless people, reminding us that they are all someone's relative, just like us.

It looks like the resolve of Lynn Nottage to deeply understand others:

> I think one of the ultimate goals of theater is to build empathy. You can invite people into the space of another for two hours, their living room, bedroom, or bathroom, and that communal experience can move people closer together. Certainly, my mantra when I was writing my play *Sweat* was, "replace judgment with curiosity." I pushed myself to enter the skin of characters whose experience was very removed from my own, some of whom I didn't necessarily relate to. However, I challenged myself to interrogate and understand the source of my resistance.
>
> So my exercise as a playwright was to investigate why did they hurt, and how can I explore that hurt, and how does the way in which they hurt intersect with my life? *Sweat* became this exercise of entering and exploring the

different ways we hurt and process our pain, whether we're black, we're white, or we're Latino.

It looks like you and me every day. It looks like us when we pull out of rigid characterizations and take the time to know ourselves and to truly look at and listen to one another. *It looks like the truth of how things are.*

PRACTICE: LOVINGKINDNESS MEDITATION FOR OURSELVES AND OTHERS

IN THIS PRACTICE, it's good to be comfortable, whether you're sitting or lying down. You can close your eyes or not. And begin the offering of lovingkindness to yourself, using the phrases from the end of chapter 5, this shortened version, or others that are meaningful to you:

May I be safe.
May I be happy.
May I be healthy.
May I live with ease.

Repeat the phrases with enough space and enough silence so that it's pleasing to you. Gather all of your attention behind one phrase at a time. If you find your attention wandering, don't worry about it. You can simply let go and begin again.

Feelings may come and go, memories may come and go. Allow them to arise and pass away. Here, the touchstone is the repetition of the phrases. You don't have to block anything else, and you don't have to follow after it.

May I be safe.
May I be happy.
May I be healthy.
May I live with ease.

Call to mind someone who's helped you, who's been good to you, or kind to you, or maybe you've never met them but they've inspired you. If someone like that comes to mind, bring them here. You can get an image of them, say their name to yourself, get a feeling for their presence, and offer the phrases of lovingkindness to them—wishing for them just what it is you've wished for yourself.

May you be safe.
May you be happy.
May you be healthy.
May you live with ease.

Even if the words don't fit totally, it doesn't matter. They're the conduits of your heart; they're the vehicle for connection.

May you be safe.
May you be happy.
May you be healthy.
May you live with ease.

You can let thoughts, emotions, and memories arise and pass away, without clinging to them, without condemning them. Maybe you have the thought *What does she need me for? She's so great,* or *What does he need me for? He's so great.* Just let it come and go. Your attention can steady on the repetition of the phrases.

And call to mind someone you know who's hurting, who's having a difficult time right now. Bring them here. You can get an image of them, say their name to yourself, get a feeling for their presence, and offer the phrases of lovingkindness to them.

May you be safe.

May you be happy.

May you be healthy.

May you live with ease.

If you find your attention wandering, you needn't be discouraged; just gently let go and come back, one phrase at a time.

Call to mind someone you might encounter now and then, a neighbor, a checkout person at the supermarket, someone you don't really know, perhaps you don't even know their name, the first person like that who comes to mind. (We call this a neutral person.) And bring them here. Even not knowing their story, you can know they want to be happy just as you do, that they're vulnerable to pain or loss just as you are, and you can wish them well.

May you be safe.

May you be happy.

May you be healthy.

May you live with ease.

And then turn toward all beings everywhere, all people, all creatures, all those in existence, known and unknown, near and far.

May all beings be safe.

May all beings be happy.

May all beings be healthy.

May all beings live with ease.

Connect to the boundlessness of life, in all directions.

May all beings be safe.

May all beings be happy.
May all beings be healthy.
May all beings live with ease.

When you feel ready, you can open your eyes. Pay attention throughout the day to see how this meditation practice may be having an effect.

7

SEEING MORE CLEARLY

✳

ONE OF THE MIND'S FEATURES, as we discussed in the previous chapter, is its tendency toward bias, a way we have of distancing ourselves from others. We might be firm in our conviction of the importance of loving thy neighbor as thyself. We might recite it and exhort others to follow that adage. And deep down, we feel it's right. But maybe we are afraid of our neighbor. Maybe we've never said hello to them, let alone loved them. Maybe we're often distancing ourselves from others and don't even notice how.

Mahzarin Banaji is a social scientist, a leader in studying implicit bias: how thoughts and feelings that reside outside our conscious awareness affect our judgments. She is co-author of the book *Blindspot: Hidden Biases of Good People*. In the book, Dr. Banaji poses a riddle I remember very well from when I was young. The riddle goes: A father and his son were in a car accident. The father dies at the scene. The boy, badly injured, is rushed to a local hospital. In the hospital, the operating surgeon looks at the boy and says, "I can't operate on this boy. He's my son." How can this be if the father just died?

I remember grappling with the riddle, feeling mystified, frustrated by the tortured mental gymnastics I tried. I remember complaining, "I hate riddles."

In her 2016 interview with Krista Tippett for the podcast *On Being*, Banaji describes her own reaction: "When I was asked this riddle in 1985, my answer was, 'Oh, the father who died at the scene was the adoptive father, and then the father who was the surgeon was the biological father.' Now, this answer is so convoluted compared to what is the actually correct answer that it boggles my mind that I did not get the right answer. So I put this riddle up on a website recently, asked lots of people. Today, 80 percent of people who read this riddle do not know the right answer. Eighty percent."

The riddle's answer is simply that the surgeon is the child's mother. Banaji goes on to say: "How could this be that I didn't get this answer?"

Many, perhaps most, of the people who wrestle with this riddle could otherwise sincerely assert that women make fine doctors, wonderful surgeons. But somehow, below the level of conscious thought, we make an assumption that defies the world as it is. (I did read one charming account, however, of a five-year-old responding, "Of course, it is the boy's *other* father," which even further challenges the culture-wide layers of assumption.)

Banaji continued her conversation with Tippett about the riddle: "Now think about this. There's something odd about the mind . . . If 100 percent of surgeons were men, this would not be a bias. This would be a fact. I've talked to doctors who work in hospitals where 80 percent of the entering class of surgeons are women. And *they* don't get the right answer. That's what you mean by 'monolith.' What is it about our minds that doesn't allow us to get to an obvious right answer?"

She goes on to say that the stereotype is like a firewall sitting in our minds. I would concur, and as a meditation teacher and a longtime meditator, I would also heartily support her observation that "there is something odd about the mind."

Odd, indeed. Look at how often we silently label others and plug them into categories of our own devising. Look at how commonly we fabricate stories about others based on little or no information, or very old information. This is how our species tries to manage the world around us. Yet we can also see that if we automatically and perpetually fear strangers, or dismiss potential friends, or hurt others because we're not aware of ways we are lost to stereotypes, we are in the grip of a hurtful and damaging habit.

While this habit of erecting mental firewalls may provide us with a fleeting sense of control in a chaotic world, it also restricts our sense of identity and narrows our experience of life. We start to inhabit a world of mental projections, filled with shadows and ghosts bred in the mind. In other words, we're brainwashed by our knee-jerk reactivity. We live in a small, cramped world of our own making.

In the United States—and in many places around the world—

we are reminded almost daily of the way assumptions about race intersect with judgment in our lives. Anurag Gupta talks about the massive disparities in how care is delivered to patients of color compared to others. On average, he says, "doctors prescribe lower doses of pain medications to darker-skinned patients, even when the patients are exhibiting the same symptoms and expressing the same pain thresholds." Somewhere there lurks a deep assumption that perhaps, Anurag says, "darker skin can withstand more pain." No doctor would say they consciously believe this but, Anurag points out, that's the nature of implicit bias. It perpetuates absurd mythologies that even a small amount of examination would reveal as wrong.

Of course, not all assumptions are wrong. We rely on assumptions informed by fact. But it's vitally important that we hold assumptions up to the light, because there are real consequences of mindlessly living by them. Sometimes deadly consequences, such as when a police officer assumes that a black teenager holding something must have a gun in his hand.

One of our more prevalent patterns of assumption is *attribution error*, which Robert Wright, author of *Why Buddhism Is True: The Science and Philosophy of Meditation and Enlightenment*, describes as follows:

> If people we identify as members of our tribe do something bad—if they're mean to someone, say, or they break the law—we tend to attribute the behavior to "situational" factors. They had been under stress at work, or they were pressured by bad actors into misbehaving, or whatever. If members of the enemy tribe do something bad, we're more

likely to explain the behavior in "dispositional" terms—the bad behavior emanates from their basic disposition, their character. It's just the kind of thing that people like them do.

Notice how each seems to call for a different remedy when something goes wrong. In one case, we forgive and seek to help. In the other, we punish and shun. And yet the behavior we're responding to is exactly the same.

If we look, we will likely see many types of assumptions we make about others, assumptions that hold us back, hold us apart, that cause pain to ourselves and that clearly cause pain to others.

TO SEE MORE CLEARLY

MINDFULNESS MEDITATION CAN help dissolve the grip of habits like stereotyping and attribution bias, leading to a cleaner, clearer view of what we are encountering, and of various possible resolutions. A principle of mindfulness training is that clearly seeing our assumptions will deconstruct them. With mindfulness we can observe our assumptions as thoughts upon their first arising, instead of noticing them only after they have driven us to action. We then have room enough to question our assumptions instead of filling all mental space with reactivity, holding on to those thoughts and building an entire projected reality upon them. With mindfulness, we also learn to view assumptions as fluid and not fixed.

A writer friend of mine was once shocked to realize how often he quickly and unconsciously sizes up another person. This realization came up at a restaurant following a talk he'd just given at a midwestern university. He was enjoying a meal with friends when a woman approached their table. My friend recalls:

> She was rather frumpy looking. I automatically assumed she lived in a rural area, probably on a farm. I also pegged her as someone who hadn't had much education. She told me how she'd come to the lecture, and my heart sank. What could her response possibly be? I wondered. She went on to say that she had enjoyed it, especially the part about Proust. I thanked her and was turning back to my friends when she blew my preconceptions right out the window. This plain-looking woman, about whom I had rushed to judgment, announced that although she thinks there are some decent translations, she much prefers reading *Remembrance of Things Past* in the original French.

There is plenty in this interaction to be mindful of. His thoughts: *She looks badly educated.* His emotions and his body: *My heart sank . . .* How learning of her mastery of a foreign language immediately changed his perception of her worth.

Mindfulness doesn't entail uptight self-scrutiny or hypervigilance, or inserting a long, awkward delay before we can say something while we inspect our thoughts and feelings. Through practice, mindfulness—which starts by working with highly focused attention—evolves into a light and natural, ever-present awareness. And it works swiftly. It's also kind; we don't have to judge ourselves for these thoughts and feelings because we realize it's our involvement with them that's the problem, not the fact that they arose to begin with. We learn to let go.

We also might enhance and extend our mindfulness practice with habits like these (as appropriate):

- *A reminder to ourselves of what we don't, in fact, know. "She's probably poorly educated," is an example.*
- *An encouragement to cultivate curiosity about someone instead of holding to certainty born of only conjecture.*
- *A practice of differentiating an individual from group-based stereotypes.*

None of these responses is about shaming or chastising ourselves. We simply see an assumption and recognize it as a thought or feeling. We recognize it is not true or that it may not be true, and we let go of it or put it in abeyance for now as we stretch mentally to see what life looks like without it standing in the way.

Fortunately, when we're committed to addressing the stubborn injustices and seemingly intractable problems of the world *and* we are not bound by so many assumptions, we have the chance to look at deeper patterns in our minds and in how the world works. We have the space to cultivate insight and discernment, to break out of old habitual perceptions and take action on a different level. This is where creative efforts are born, unexpected collaborations are nurtured, rigid time lines are disrupted, and actions based on a greater vision of interconnectedness can find support.

EXPLORE THE CAUSES AND CONDITIONS

ONCE ON A visit to the Insight Meditation Society in Barre, Thai activist Sulak Sivaraksa was asked how to combat the sex trade in Thailand. He replied, "If you want to really affect the sex trade, look at Thai agricultural policy." In other words, look deeper. He went on to say, "There is a reason those farmers are selling their children. They are starving. Why?"

A lifelong Buddhist practitioner, Sivaraksa was urging us to look at causes and conditions that lie beneath this terrible problem, going as deep as we could go, to find responses that might actually make a more fundamental difference. I took from that evening the intention to look more consciously for causes and conditions so that the love and compassion I try to develop, the good-heartedness I cultivate, can be joined with clarity and creative vision about where to try to make change.

An old story from the Buddhist tradition drives home this point about how compassionate action involves looking deeply at causes and conditions. The Buddha was talking to a king and suggested to him, "You should be just. You should be fair. You should be generous." The king remembered the first two points but forgot to be generous, so people in the kingdom began to go hungry and started stealing. The king focused on punishing thieves. In response, the Buddha pointed out that the way forward is not to start making laws against theft; the way forward is to look at why people are hungry.

I've witnessed the extraordinary impact that incorporating an understanding of causes and conditions into social justice strategies can have. Take Wangari Maathai, the Kenyan zoology professor and grassroots organizer who saw the link between an increasingly depleted environment and the impoverishment of her people.

"If you destroy the forest," Maathai observed, "then the river will stop flowing, the rains will become irregular, the crops will fail, and you will die of hunger and starvation."

She started the Green Belt Movement in the late 1970s, a confederation of community groups that has, over the years, planted more than fifty-one million trees. The trees help to stem erosion, produce food and firewood, and create habitat and livelihoods. For this and her other conservation work in the face of political opposition, Maathai received the Nobel Peace Prize in 2004. She died in 2011, but the Green Belt Movement carries on.

For anyone working in the realm of social change, where suffering can seem intractable, tackling what seem to be the underlying causes of a particular problem is valuable. Otherwise, we may feel like we're running in place. For example, those working to ease poverty often see it as a symptom of a deeper problem—such as the denial of basic rights to certain groups, such as women. Bhikkhu Bodhi, the Buddhist monk we met in chapter 1 who helped to form an aid organization called Buddhist Global Relief, talked with me about his work in searching for causes and conditions in trying to address poverty:

One thing we came to see, in dealing with hunger and malnutrition, is that it's not sufficient just to provide direct food aid to those in need. We realized it's necessary to look for the underlying roots of hunger, malnutrition, and poverty. As we were investigating these issues, one of the things that we kept coming across is the way chronic hunger and malnutrition are connected to the subordinate status of girls and women in many traditional cultures. Consequently, we came to understand that one of the most effective ways to rectify the problem of hunger and malnutrition is by promoting the status of girls and women—by providing girls with education, which would widen their social and economic opportunities, and by helping women receive training that would equip them to set up their own livelihood projects.

Dan Vexler of the Freedom Fund, a global philanthropic initiative to end modern slavery, wrote in the *Stanford Social Innovation Review* about using something called *systems thinking* in working for social change: "In the fight against slavery, a systems change approach might address weak rule of law, harmful attitudes toward women or certain ethnic groups, or irresponsible business practices—in contrast to a narrower approach that focuses on, say, rescuing victims. This is how we tend to use the term at the Freedom Fund, and it underlines the importance we place on preventing people from falling into situations of slavery in the first place."

SEEING THE SYSTEMS AT WORK

WHEN I FIRST came across the notion of systems change in this context, I was intrigued. It felt like a shift that could potentially make a big difference. If we look for rock-bottom essential causes, we might be tempted to say greed, hatred, delusion, evil, or human nature—however, the deepest roots of harm are expressed in our moral codes, philosophies, religious tenets, and beliefs. But we're also looking for root causes at a level that is actionable in a social context, not merely the philosophical underpinnings to our worldview. One single cause is extremely difficult (if not impossible) to isolate in complex systems, so in the effort to create change, we must consider the interconnections among the many causes we can identify.

Writer Rebecca Solnit is a fierce defender of the environment who fights many of her battles on the page. She's not one to shy away from hard truths, as in the essay "When the Hero Is the Problem," which she wrote for *Literary Hub*. In it, she noted our tendency to hang hopes and expectations on a single savior with a magic cure rather than expand our thinking and efforts more deeply:

> Even the idea that the solution will be singular and dramatic and in the hands of one person erases that the solutions to problems are often complex and many faceted and arrived at via negotiations. The solution to climate change is planting trees but also transitioning (rapidly) away from fossil fuels but also energy efficiency and significant design changes but also a dozen more things about soil and agriculture and transportation and how systems work. There is no solution, but there are many pieces that add up to a solution, or rather to a modulation of the problem of climate change.

Certainly, our passions, our responsibilities, and our time commitments might lead us to focus on the issue we are most moved by, rather than trying to address the world's every ill. And devoting ourselves to one issue or one remedy might well bring about the most effective and meaningful course of action in some instances. But if we bring a broad perspective to the forefront of anything we do, we will extend and bolster the compassion we develop. Our actions can align with the clearest, most inclusive truth we can uncover.

David DeSteno, a psychology professor at Northeastern University, led a study of whether mindfulness practice resulted in acts of compassion using two groups of subjects: one that had done eight weeks of meditation training and a group with no meditation experience. Here's how he set it up: Sitting in a staged waiting room with three chairs were two actors. With one empty chair left, the participant sat down and waited to be called. Another actor using crutches and appearing to be in great physical pain, would then enter the room. As she did, the actors in the chair would ignore her by fiddling with their phones or opening a book.

Would the subjects who took part in the meditation classes be more likely to come to the aid of the person in pain, even in the face of everyone else ignoring her? And indeed, the results bore that out, leading the researchers to posit a link between mindfulness meditation and compassion: among the non-meditating participants, only about 15 percent of people acted to help. But among the participants who were in the meditation sessions, "we were able to boost that up to 50 percent," said DeSteno.

Acts of generosity and kindness are the vital, day-to-day, moment-to-moment channels of transformation. We badly need more of them as this world splinters into hyper-partisanship and infectious ill will. It can also be helpful to recognize the value of thinking in terms of systems change even as we might be focused on acts of personal goodness. We rely on analysis and conscious reflection to make that distinction. When I heard of DeSteno's experiment, it made me think in terms of systems. I wondered, for example, if anyone questioned how the people running the lab were allocating resources if they were putting so few chairs in their waiting room?

I have experienced over and over how mindfulness meditation brings forth compassion. Countless times, a new meditator has come up to me and said something like, "A street person asked me for money, and my automatic habit has been to give a few dollars. This was the first time I looked the street person in the eyes and realized that they were a human being."

That realization is genuine and unforced, not a result of trying to seem "spiritual" or "perfect." The power of such a connection can't really be overstated. And yet, this person may not go on to reflect, *I wonder what the housing policy is in this city.*

To think in that way, involving whole systems, is often based on a certain kind of training. We look not just deeper but wider. That ability to consider a bigger picture of influences and elements coming together to form this moment gives us not only discernment but a more expansive space for creative expression, whether we are trying to help one person or change a policy. One of the core tenets of the Holistic Life Foundation is expressed in its motto: Look at the Whole, Not Just the Parts. As HLF's three founders work with individuals intimately within the Baltimore school system, they also work for systemic change at the level of the school, the city, the state, the country, and the world, which is one of the reasons they chose *holistic* as a key word in the name of their organization.

NETWORK LOOKING

JUST AS WE practiced looking at a tree or a piece of paper differently to sense interconnectedness in chapter 6, we can use what we could call *network looking* (carefully observing a web of interrelationships) to remind ourselves of the many constituent elements going into an experience, and in doing so, we bring alive a bigger, more inclusive picture.

In day-to-day life, this translates into a much more realistic perception of the larger patterns and confluences we are all a part of. Consider for a moment the shirt you are wearing . . . the materials, grown or spun . . . the labor of many hands to weave or sew the garment . . . the process by which you came to own it. Through the use of active imagination, this kind of reflection brings us to realize, "There is a great deal of life embodied in this shirt. It's not just an object or commodity."

If we only see objects—a shirt—there's a perception of inflexibility, even intractability in our world. By contrast, as I've been suggesting, we can practice looking in terms of networks or systems, which could be especially useful in looking at a nexus of suffering in a society. In looking in this way, breaking down what might at first have seemed static and monolithic into constituent parts, we also ignite a sense of dynamism and change. That's why it doesn't feel more oppressive to consider a problem in this way—it feels freeing. We see life pulsating within any object, any system.

The dynamics of the moon's gravitational influence upon earthly bodies of water are such that the waters, except in rare instances, will act in concord. The tides come and affect the water level in the ocean and then in the rivers, then in the smaller streams. With the tide, the great ocean swells, and the river swells, and when the river swells, the smaller rivers in the delta will swell. When the ocean ebbs, the rivers will ebb and the smaller rivers will ebb. With the arising of one thing, there is the arising of another thing connected to it, conditioned by it. Nothing in life stands alone.

In an ecosystem, various elements—the animals, plants, water, terrain—make up an interconnected, dynamic structure. Think about how many transport systems and communications systems you've utilized today and how the different components rely on one another. A change to one element affects the entire system. From this vantage point, interdependence is seen as the very fabric of every experience. A systems approach tends to focus on the relationships, structures, and feedback loops that make up the whole. That way we are constantly learning, seeing the problem as an ever-changing process.

WHAT AREN'T WE SEEING?

MORE THAN A decade ago, I was at a conference about love and social justice. One afternoon, there was a presentation by someone who was going into prisons in Texas to hold literacy classes. They told several moving stories of people whose lives had been turned around by learning to read. I could well believe it. As a child, reading had been my salvation, the public library my strongest refuge. And I know how difficult it can be to go into a prison to teach. In most cases, it's a soul-killing atmosphere designed to be the opposite of enlivening for anyone who walks through those gates.

Then Rev. Sam Mann stood up. Rev. Mann was a white minister with an African American congregation in Kansas City. "I'm wondering," he stated, "if you have ever investigated the terrible racism that pervades the criminal justice system in Texas, that sends so many of those men and women to prison to begin with."

This was a powerful moment for me. While I felt great respect for the first speaker, who described leading classes in some awful circumstances he was not obliged to volunteer for, I also realized Rev. Mann was describing a prevalent pattern that, when

I overlooked it, severely limited my understanding. There may be many strong contributing elements to a situation that we are oblivious to because they don't tend to touch us directly. There's quite a lot each of us is trained to take for granted. There's quite a lot each of us fails to notice. I realized that my action becomes a very different action when I commit to the big picture: Look at the Whole, Not Just the Parts.

MINDFULNESS AND CLEAR COMPREHENSION

THE WORD *SATI* from the Pali language (the original language of the Buddha) is usually translated as *mindfulness*. When I was studying in India, the term was most often used as part of a compound, *sati-sampajanna*, which means mindfulness *and* clear comprehension. The *sati* part (mindfulness) is sometimes called *bare attention*, a single-pointed awareness of what is happening to us and in us, without falling sway to interpretation, to holding on or pushing away. It allows us to observe our experience with fresh eyes.

We build on that open and free perception—not trying to confirm a belief, advance an agenda, or manipulate our experience—and develop wisdom, or clear comprehension, the *sampajanna* part. Classically, clear comprehension refers to analyses like, "Is the action I'm intending really in accord with my purpose in life?"

Deciding that an action is ill advised could come out of the greatest compassion for ourselves. We might discern, "I originally thought that was such a formidable way to speak to my opponent. Look at how much fear is laced throughout that act. Look at the residue all this time later."

We look at purpose. We look at motivation. We look at the difference between reality and what we might have been taught. Is vengefulness all that satisfying, really? Is compassion actually weak? Am I as alone and in control as I've always thought? It's not just a question of intellectual probing for curiosity's sake to ask these questions; it's a spur to come closer to our experience and observe for ourselves what seems to be true.

Rhonda Magee is a professor of law at the University of San Francisco who uses mindfulness in classes and workshops to facilitate racial understanding. In her work, Rhonda provides excellent and timely forms of inquiry into interconnections, causes, and conditions.

I've thought a lot about what up-to-date inquiry and analysis leading to clear comprehension might look like. In that light, I've adapted a practice of conscious reflection from Rhonda's book, *The Inner Work of Racial Justice*, to be found at the end of this chapter on page 191.

This application of mindfulness is distinct from intently focusing on developing concentration or one-pointedness. It works with cultivating the broader awareness, the kind of "network looking," the clear comprehension (*sampajanna*) we've been looking at.

WHO IS PATROLLING THE BORDERS OF REALITY?

IT'S EASY TO overlook the question of whose perspective is central and defining versus whose is marginalized—especially if we think of *ourselves* as being at the center, a point of reference that just seems "normal" to us. Our perspective simply expresses reality for us, and our assumption is that it expresses reality altogether and for everyone.

Interestingly, when I spent time in a hospital in 2019, I had many male nurses. I can remember one who pretty much always identified himself as a "male nurse," instead of simply a "nurse." Somehow, he needed a qualifier. And in a time when gender fluidity is becoming more pronounced, requiring a qualifying term is likely only to get more complex. You can tell the world is changing when the qualifiers drop away and language changes, indicating our conceptual framework has been shaken.

Sulak Sivaraksa started me down the path of looking with more vigor at causes and conditions. Ever since the moment when Rev. Mann stood up at that conference and asked whether we had considered the deeper causes of the prisoners' situation, I try to look at a more inclusive, system-wide range of influences and conditions. This has led me to reflect on some hard questions, sit with some uncomfortable feelings, listen more, and step out of the box when considering what actions I might take. Hence my comments about those chairs in the DeSteno lab waiting room. What about if, in addition to cultivating good-heartedness through mindfulness and other means, we were trained to apply analysis to any system we're looking at, to engage in network seeing and deeper inquiry of the kind Rhonda Magee does with her students?

Ellen Agler, CEO of the END Fund, working to eliminate neglected tropical diseases, talked to me about taking one's awareness beneath the surface of the immediate problems you're addressing:

Pretty much across any political spectrum, any cultural perspective, people can rally around the idea that kids should not grow up with hundreds of worms in their bellies absorbing nutrients. Or people should not have to go blind by the age of thirty because they were bitten by infected flies and contracted river blindness. But I think those of us involved in social action in developing countries need to realize that there's a legacy here we have to be very aware of—with histories affected by colonialism, paternalism, exploitation, and "othering" of many types—that could easily crop up unintentionally.

Sometimes *how* you solve a problem is as important as solving it. Mindfulness has taught me how to stay with the conversations that have the scary potential to shift the whole way I see myself or the way I'm working. It has given me the willingness to question the ways we can collaborate. It has given me the sense that this moment, every moment, is history turning all around and through us. We are being called to wake up and recognize our actions in the context of both a moment and in the context of how history has unfolded over centuries at the same time.

CREATIVE COLLABORATION

I'VE SAT IN discharge planning meetings for a friend getting ready to leave a psychiatric hospital after a long stay; meetings about working in Syrian refugee camps; meetings for a candidate's political campaign; meetings about changes in zoning laws; and countless other highly charged meetings involving engaged people who care about things that matter. It usually becomes apparent, whatever the scope of the work, who is the kind of leader who thinks outside the box, and who works to bring other participants together rather than singularly shine themselves. It also becomes apparent how valuable that kind of leadership is.

When dealing with large-scale change, a common term these days for that valued leadership is *system entrepreneur.* A system entrepreneur is someone who seeks to address social needs by drawing upon the strengths and assets of diverse actors in a system, inspiring creative collaboration. They help like-minded organizations and individuals focus on a problem of shared concern, like the eradication of malaria, or educational innovation—and act among the members of the coalition to help bring forth each one's capabilities and resources.

And those feedback loops among those who are coalescing around an issue are key. A systems approach helps shift us from formulaic, mechanical responses to issues to fluid responses that see the interconnected and constantly changing elements that keep emerging.

I've become fascinated by this idea, whether one is trying to effect change at the level of an individual, a family, a community, or a country facing a crisis. I think of the open-mindedness and agility needed to maintain a big vision and also be able to pivot from the path one is on to one that may be more creative. And I think of what I have heard philanthropist Jeff Walker—a leading thinker on system entrepreneurship—speak of many times as a "managed ego": you highlight collaboration rather than competition and are committed to leading by helping others work together to the very best of their ability toward a common goal. Given fierce competition for resources, including in the worlds of doing good, we need all the creativity, cooperation, and systems thinking we can muster.

Erica Ford is co-founder and CEO of LIFE Camp, which provides youth impacted by violence tools to stay in school and out of the criminal justice system. LIFE Camp—which includes a team that specializes in interrupting violence by mediating conflicts and de-escalating gun incidents—works in some of New York City's most underserved communities. They build relationships with young people who feel they have nothing to look forward to. They listen deeply.

Here is how Erica responded when I asked her about her work and her experience of violence as a public health issue:

Let's look at a typical young kid we'll call Michael. Inside his house is domestic violence. Outside his house, somebody got shot last night. They got the yellow tape, the chalk outline, cones for the bullets. He continues past that on his daily walk to school. Then he sees a gang fight going on up the block. He sees a girl cursing out a guy. He goes into the classroom, and the teacher's talking and he's not paying attention. And then somebody hits up next to him, maybe to get his attention, and Michael punches him in the face.

Michael gets suspended for 180 days and put into another school with a bunch of people like him who never got help. They're sitting there in a cesspool of poison and infecting one another with their disease of violence. But nobody is getting looked at as a human being with health issues. Nobody is getting diagnosed, looking at what happened to this kid and why did he respond like that? And what happened to his mother? And what happened to his father? And what happened to his grandmother? And why is this cycle of violence and irrational behaviors and irrational decisions happening in Michael's life and community? Nobody is looking at the treatment: What can we do to transform these vicious cycles he is caught in? Instead, we're asking how many years can we lock him up or how many days can we suspend him—as if we don't know that suspending him will just make him come back even more mad with his emotional wounds untended to?

We're instilling cultures and conditions and beliefs that breed separation, not interconnection. Why can't Medicaid consider yoga as medicine, or LIFE Camp as medicine, or going on a nature retreat as medicine? We have to shift how we look at violence, how we put people in buckets and brackets and hold them there for their entire life because they made one mistake at sixteen or seventeen. We cannot do that to people. We can't.

Viewing violence as a public health problem is a perfect living example of the adage attributed to Albert Einstein: "We can't solve significant problems by using the same kind of thinking we used when we created them." If we are willing to experiment with expanding how we pay attention and deepening and broadening our inquiry, I believe we have the chance to arrive at a different level of thinking. With the insights we derive from that, we can take big steps toward solving some of the deepest problems and reducing some of the most egregious forms of suffering we see in our world.

PRACTICE: AWARENESS OF THE EMBODIED SELF

Lovingkindness for the You the World Sees

Take a few minutes to bring your attention to your body in this moment. Gently focus on your experience of this very moment. Get granular: Notice the subtle sensations of breathing in and out, including the points of contact between your body and the ground beneath you. Rest in the strength of these grounding sensations.

Now call to mind one aspect of your outward identity that other people notice by sight or sound alone when they encounter you. This might be your gender, your age, or what you may think of as your ethnicity—aspects of language and culture that are part of how you identify yourself in the world.

Home in on this aspect of who you appear to be.

Consider how this affects how you are received, what opportunities may be available to you, whether you are given the benefit of the doubt.

Pause and notice what thoughts, emotions, or sensations are arising in you right now.

What were you taught to believe about bodies like yours? About differently racialized bodies?

How might this aspect of your social identity have shaped your experience in the world? Have you spent more time in places where you were in a significant minority or majority based on your race or gender?

Are there ways that this identity has been a source of comfort to you? A source of advantage to you?

Are there ways that this identity has been a source of discomfort to you? A source of disadvantage to you?

Then, practice letting your thoughts (judgments, stories) go. Imagine each as a cloud floating across a blue sky, and return to the sensations of the body and the breath.

8

EXQUISITE BALANCE

✳

How do we navigate the overall unruliness of life, so filled as it is with urgencies—tasks left undone, friends who need help, health problems, financial pressures, family crises, community crises, world crises? How do we sustain ourselves, our sanity, our open hearts and clear vision in the face of these ongoing challenges? In Buddhist psychology, the answer is equanimity.

When I think of equanimity, I turn to the Pali word *upekkha,* which is most effectively translated as *balance,* often the balance born from wisdom. For some, the word *equanimity* implies coolness, indifference, or even fear masquerading as being "just fine." A teenager shrugging and saying, "Whatever," is a perfect example of that particular impression of equanimity. It feels mean, doesn't it, as you're trying to offer care or help, to be met with a "Whatever"?

Another idea that people presume for the meaning of equanimity is passivity. In that view, if you approach bad things with equanimity, maybe you're just a doormat being walked on or a dry leaf asking to be blown about by the winds of change.

The word *balance* itself can also be misunderstood. Sometimes it's dismissed as a forced or constrained state achieved through valiantly propping something up (like cheerfulness) while simultaneously pushing something else down (like sorrow). Or holding both pleasure and pain in a tight fist, hoping the pain doesn't leap out of your hand to take over. Balance is readily seen as mediocrity, something bland, a series of concessions that takes you to the lowest common denominator.

A few years ago, I was in a marketing meeting related to a program I was involved in at the Garrison Institute. For four years, we had offered yoga and meditation as resilience skills for frontline workers in domestic violence shelters. At that point, the program was exploring expanding that skills training to international humanitarian aid workers, which required rewriting all of the material, so we gathered to talk about how to do that.

I tried to explain the changes I had seen the frontline workers go through during the program, and I found myself apologizing: "I know it's not an exciting word or a compelling word—it can easily sound kind of boring—but an enormous benefit described by them was an increase in balance."

At that point, every one of the marketing team members laughed. "You know who really likes the word *balance*?" one of them asked. "Anyone who feels out of balance. That's a lot of people!"

FEELING INTENSITY WITHOUT BEING OVERWHELMED

THE KIND OF balance I'm talking about is not a measurement of how much time you spend doing one thing and then another, trying to create equality between them. Instead, it has to do with having perspective on life, and the effort you're putting out, and the changes you're going through. We establish this sense of balance within. It demands of us wisdom, and it gives us a growing sense of peace.

Balance doesn't come from wiping out all feeling. We don't have many models for navigating strong emotions in a more balanced way. It's an uncommon trait. Many of us are conditioned toward extremes. When it comes to feeling painful emotions like anger, we may get lost in them, such that they become toxic and seemingly inescapable. We may think there's no way out, and we come to identify with our feelings completely: *I'm an angry person, and I always will be.*

On the other hand, we may tend to feel an impulse to turn away from tough feelings—to swallow them, deny them, distract ourselves. Whether we're drowning in these painful emotions or pushing them away, it's still putting pain on top of pain.

Equanimity is what frees us from these dynamics; we can learn to be present with emotions without falling into the extremes of overwhelm or denial. Equanimity is the state in which we can recognize an emotion like anger—and even feel its full intensity—but also pay attention to choosing how we will respond to a given feeling, thought, or circumstance.

One of my favorite illustrations of this phenomenon comes from Andrés Gonzaléz of the Holistic Life Foundation, whom we first met in chapter 3. He told me the story of eight-year-old Janaisa, one of the girls in the after-school program they run, who had a history of getting into fights with her peers. "Boys or girls, it didn't matter, they would make fun of her and she'd knock them out," he says. But then one day in the gym, when another girl made a disparaging remark about her, Janaisa grabbed her and slammed her against the wall. "She then silently looked at the girl," recalled Andrés, "and then dropped her, saying, 'You'd better be glad I meditate.'"

We can choose not to make an enemy of our feelings, as intense as they may be. Instead, we can expand our awareness and allow those feelings to come up. And we can allow them to move and shift. That space brings the wisdom that keeps us from getting lost in immediate reactivity. That freedom is the essence of equanimity.

A LIVING GYROSCOPE

BEFORE I BEGAN meditating, when I thought of being out of balance, I would visualize a hand holding an old-fashioned scale, where one of the weighted brass plates was a bit lower than the other. But that image didn't quite capture the way I actually felt when what I needed was some equanimity.

As life twists and turns, often we try to convey the impression that we've got it all together. But sometimes we maintain the appearance of steadiness only by staying in a state of tension so high that our emotional equilibrium can be blown off course by the mildest of breezes. Is it truly a life in balance if it requires so much effort? Ease is part of what we want: to feel unrestricted, peaceful, and free, to be able to respond appropriately to our world as it changes.

I've come to think that a better image for balance is a gyroscope. The gyroscope is a wonderful visual representation of equanimity: the ability to find calm and steadiness under stress. That balance is loose and limber, capable of ducking some of what's coming and getting quickly back to true.

Watch a gyroscope in motion and you'll see the wonder of the simple way it maintains a perfect balance. The core of the gyroscope, its axis, spins with such power that it keeps the big circle around it well balanced. Although constantly in motion, the gyroscope is stable, adjusting to whatever comes its way. A gust of wind or a hard knock on the table will send a spinning top tumbling, but not a gyroscope. Try to knock it over and it gracefully and steadily rights itself.

As we navigate through circumstances, we can learn to be more agile and responsive instead of reactive. The balance of a gyroscope comes from its strong core—its central, stable energy. A sense of meaning in our lives can give us that core, lifting our aspirations, strengthening us in adversity, helping us have a sense of who we are and what we care about in spite of changing situations.

The Upaya Zen Center co-abbot we first met in chapter 6, Joshin, talked to me about growing up in Brooklyn in a poor family with an alcoholic father and how he found a strong enough center to get him through:

I had these Catholic roots. Even as a young kid, I took a lot of comfort in the images of Saint Francis, the pauper, and Jesus, who loved outcasts. Those stories always moved me a lot. Somehow, I could identify with them. Religious life offered me what I thought was a way out. When I joined the Dominicans, the vow of poverty was a step up for me. I entered the Dominicans with ten dollars in my pocket, and you had to hand in all your money when you went in. And then they gave me twenty-five dollars back as my monthly stipend. So I thought, *Oh, okay, you know, I could do with twenty-five dollars a month.* In this sense, religious life was an escape—it started out as a way of finding some safety for myself. But this transformed over time. I developed a sense of spiritual self that was bigger than the hardships of my life. Religious life gave me a sense that I wasn't *just* that. Even though I left the Dominicans, as I look back at that time, it gave me a sense of meaning. It gave me a way to use my experience, to develop a life of service, to develop a life that seemed to have purpose.

Discovering (or rediscovering) a sense of purpose begins with identifying and examining our most deeply held values. When we align our actions with those values or concerns that have centering power in our lives—those we're most devoted to, that form the passionate core of what we care about—our actions are empowered, whatever the challenge.

Bernice Johnson Reagon, the singer with Sweet Honey in the Rock, was a dedicated activist in the early '60s. Recalling the danger she and her friends faced in challenging segregation in Georgia, she said, "Now I sit back and look at some of the things we did, and I say, 'What in the world came over us?' But death had nothing to do with what we were doing. If somebody shot us, we would be dead. And when people died, we cried and went to funerals. And we went and did the next thing the next day, because it was really beyond life and death. It was really like sometimes you know what you're supposed to be doing."

When we have a sense of what we are supposed to be doing and we then go out and do it, we forge a center and reinforce the core strength we can return to and rely on again and again.

We also strengthen the core within ourselves by paying attention to the perimeter of the gyroscope as much as the axis. Defining a perimeter around us means we no longer consider ourselves completely responsible for absolutely everything. Even if life events are hard, we don't have to embellish them to make them even harder: "This is going to last forever," or "This has to be worked out right now," or "This proves I'm worthless and ineffective." The wisdom of the gyroscope says, "Breathe a bit so you can act, and appreciate what comes next."

We may charge into situations imagining that maintaining control is the secret to making life work. We can affect things around us—that's the whole point of taking action—but it's not helpful to think we're going to finally be in absolute control. That's not going to happen, not even for a moment. We don't wield control over who is going to get sick, who is going to get better, or the inevitable ups and downs of our activism. We cannot immediately direct everybody and everything in this world to our liking. Would that it were so!

We might act fervently, and hopefully we would, to alleviate suffering. But to imagine that we can decide the certain outcome of our efforts is like thinking we're going to wake up in the morning one day, look in the mirror, and determine, "I've thought about it really carefully. I've weighed all the pros and cons, and I've decided I'm not going to die." The body has its own nature. Certainly, we can affect that, and we can transform a lot and be very impactful, but death is not a decision we make.

We do everything we can, and then we need to let go of our expectation and disappointment. If we don't, our fearful fantasies and shattered dreams will be endless. If we plant the seed of our effort with a willingness to do all that we can, plus the wisdom of knowing that we don't do it all ourselves and that we cannot simply command everything to our liking, we won't feel defeated by circumstances.

EQUANIMITY HOLDS EVERYTHING

EQUANIMITY CAN BE described as the voice of wisdom, being open to everything, able to hold everything. Its essence is complete presence. Very early in my teaching career, we met with retreatants in fifteen-minute personal interviews, during which time we got to hear what was happening for them and respond. I quickly recognized how meeting with four people in a row, or even two, I could be encountering people with wildly different life experiences. One time, the first person I met with was recently engaged to be married and the second was utterly traumatized, grappling with the murder of her roommate.

I saw in those early days of meeting with people and being exposed to such widely fluctuating sets of circumstances that I really would need a heart as wide as the world to accommodate the shifts of pleasure and pain being presented and to be able to accompany each of these people on their own journey with all-embracing presence. It's hard for us to allow our own or someone else's pain fully if we are afraid it will steal our possibility for joy. It's hard to allow joy its full expression if we have used it to avoid confronting the reality of pain.

The special kind of pain known as *survivor guilt* is a particularly challenging obstacle for those who have evaded terrible fates through what seems an accident of timing or birth. When you're a survivor, to want anything more than what you've got can feel outrageous and selfish. Samantha Novick, a member of the Parkland community whom we first met in chapter 2, has become well acquainted with this phenomenon. She told me that she has felt strange at times, because the various mindfulness classes and workshops that arose in the aftermath of the shooting and the sense of community that arose in response had often been amazing and exhilarating for her, and yet they came about only because of a horrific tragedy.

She asked me, "How do I move from one to the other?"

"I don't think you do," I told her. "I think we learn to hold both at the same time."

I really believe that. Equanimity holds it all. Peace is not about moving away from or transcending all the pain in order to travel to an easeful, spacious realm of relief: we cradle both the immense sorrow and the wondrousness of life at the same time. Being able to be fully present with both is the gift equanimity gives us— spacious stillness, radiant calm.

Environmental activist and author Joanna Macy—in conversation with Krista Tippett on the *On Being* podcast, said, "[If] we can be fearless, to be with our pain, it turns. It doesn't stay static.

It only doesn't change if we refuse to look at it. But when we look at it, when we take it in our hands, when we can just be with it and keep breathing, then it turns. It turns to reveal its other face, and the other face of our pain for the world is our love for the world, our absolutely inseparable connectedness with all life."

Equanimity means being with pain and pleasure, joy and sorrow, in such a way that our hearts are fully open and also whole, intact. We can recognize what is true, even if painful, and also know peace. Equanimity doesn't mean we have no feeling about anything; it's not a state of blankness. Instead, it is the spaciousness that can relate to any feeling, any occurrence, any arising, and still be free.

WHAT DOES THIS MEAN IF YOU WANT TO HAVE AN EFFECT IN THE WORLD?

IN HIS ESSAY "Notes of a Native Son," James Baldwin spoke famously and eloquently about one of life's great tensions:

It began to seem that one would have to hold in the mind forever two ideas which seemed to be in opposition. The first idea was acceptance, the acceptance, totally without rancor, of life as it is, and men as they are: in the light of this idea, it goes without saying that injustice is a commonplace. But this did not mean that one could be complacent, for the second idea was of equal power: that one must never, in one's own life, accept these injustices as commonplace but must fight them with all one's strength. This fight begins, however, in the heart and it now had been laid to my charge to keep my own heart free of hatred and despair.

Daisy Hernández is a cultural activist, an assistant professor at Miami University in Ohio, and author of the memoir *A Cup of Water Under My Bed*. Hernández wrote in *Tricycle* magazine:

I had read Baldwin's essay many times and had taught it to my students, but for the first time I saw that it is a teaching on equanimity. Acceptance means seeing a situation as it is. The winds—or hurricanes—that had been pushing me around were not just the horrors but my unspoken insistence that the horrors should not exist and that I should get to be a Buddhist during the "good" times, not these times. I heard in Baldwin's words the emphasis on holding two opposing ideas: accepting the existence of injustice and fighting to vanquish it. I heard, too, the clarion call that equanimity is my "charge," my responsibility. That it means keeping my own heart steady, free, and open.

It's hard to describe how soft my chest cavity felt when I acknowledged all this. Maybe it was my imagination, but I sensed in my body a kind of anchoring, a settling in, a sense of I see this, even this, and I felt strong, too. It's odd to say that I felt both soft and strong at the same time, but I did. I also felt renewed.

EQUANIMITY REUNITES US WITH OUR CAPACITY FOR FORBEARANCE

IT'S ONE THING to celebrate and appreciate equanimity, to understand it, but how do we cultivate it?

As the Buddha described life, he spoke of pleasure and pain, gain and loss, praise and blame, fame and disrepute, often described as "the eight worldly winds." It's just how life is. There is no one who experiences only pleasure and no pain. There is no act that elicits only praise and no blame. Appreciating this fact is not a call for apathy or depression. We can recognize the truth of things, accept them as the inevitable fabric of life, and understand that the best way to work for change is not to be freaked out, or in denial, or anxious with the ups, lest they dissolve, and plummet with the downs, fearing they won't. Equanimity implies a posture of dignity even in a whirlwind of change. It implies being able to breathe. It implies complete presence. It implies being able to come to peace.

If we take the time to reflect on the inevitable turnings of life, it will build our equanimity. If we practice fully experiencing the joy of certain moments without fearfully clinging to them, it will build equanimity. If, as Joanna Macy said earlier, we look at the pain and keep breathing, it will build equanimity. All of it will build a quality of radiant calm that is intricate, shifting, alive.

In her *Tricycle* essay, Daisy Hernández described the first time she recognized equanimity in action, during Hurricane Andrew, in 1992:

> I was a preteen, staying with my father's cousin, Margo, and her family in South Florida . . . Margo did not panic when the winds began. She boiled water. She cooked pots of black beans. She slipped her husband a sedative. When the hurricane finally ended, sparing us but killing 65 people, Margo walked us around the neighborhood to survey the damage. The hurricane had yanked giant palm trees and flipped them over, so their thick roots poked at the air

like colossal brown fingers. Margo . . . boiled more water and got us all fed, and no plate of Cuban black beans ever tasted better.

We build equanimity by pairing it with compassion. In some Buddhist literature, they use the example of an elderly person sitting in a playground, watching children play. By that age, you've likely seen a lot of change, you've had to let go of a lot. As you sit there, you see a child freaking out because they've broken a shovel. You're not cold and mean. You don't go up to the child and say, "Hey, kid, it's just a shovel! Wait until you have a real problem, like a mortgage or sciatica." Rather, you're warm, tender, kind.

At the same time, you don't fall down on the ground and sob with the child. You have the perspective of wisdom. "You know what? Shovels break." Everything can break. Relationships break. Carefully nurtured plans break. Hearts certainly break. Life can get very hard. You know the poignancy of that in the cells of your body by the time you are of an age, and so you're able to maintain some spaciousness in your mind with the ups and downs. Not icy distance but spaciousness. That spacious stillness is equanimity.

I know if I reach out for help from someone, I certainly don't want them to respond with meanness, "Hey, that's just a shovel." But at the same time, if they fell down on the ground sobbing, "Things are irredeemably bad!" I'd be terrified. I definitely want to receive compassion and at the same time, even if it isn't in words but in the look in someone's eye, to sense there is some outlook that is possible that isn't completely shaped by my heartache or disappointment.

There are meditation practices where we call someone to mind and silently repeat phrases that bring together warmth and spaciousness, caring and the acknowledgment of our limits. "I care about your pain, and I can't control it." That is combining compassion and equanimity. That's what those phrases are meant to convey—that we do and should and must open our hearts and care and connect and dedicate our lives to the alleviation of suffering *and yet* understand that things happen as they happen.

In Buddhist psychology when we talk about certain qualities like compassion, we consider what the "near enemy" of that beneficial state might be. A near enemy is a quality that can masquerade as the one we want to cultivate. The near enemy of compassion is overwhelm or despair. These days, we would call it *burnout*. We recognize the suffering that exists, so there is clarity, but the pain we recognize permeates our being and we are overcome. Then we can't serve anyone, Buddhist teachings say—and my experience bears this out. Equanimity *balances* our caring so that compassionate action can be sustained and we don't drown under the weight of our sorrow.

WITH EQUANIMITY, WE TAKE ACTION

RACHEL GUTTER, THE environmental activist we first met in chapter 5, recalls that after the U.S. presidential election in 2016, she was exhibiting signs of hypervigilance: "I would hear a loud sound in the middle of the night and sit bolt upright and the first thought I would have is, *Oh, my God, North Korea is bombing us.* I didn't stay in that place of hair-trigger fear, though. And it's my work that allows me not to sit in that place. Because I'm taking action. Because I'm doing the best that I can and doing the most that I can and having a sense that this place that I am in right now is the place where I can contribute the most."

WITH EQUANIMITY, WE DON'T TAKE *EVERY* ACTION

ANURAG GUPTA, THE breaking-bias expert we've met in several chapters, talked to me about how he maintains boundaries when he's asked to help a particular cause: "For me, it's not that I'm ignoring them. I'm not saying that they're not important, but I know my purpose in life. I know what my passion is. I know what makes me happy. I want to move in that direction and not have to worry about taking care of everything else and everybody else."

CROSSING THE FLOOD OF SUFFERING

REFERRING TO THE flood of suffering, someone once asked the Buddha, "How did you, Lord Buddha, cross the flood?"

And the Buddha replied, "Without lingering, friend, and without hurrying across the flood."

And then the question came, "But how did you, without lingering, without hurrying, cross the flood?"

The Buddha replied, "Friend, when I lingered, then I sank; when I hurried, I was swept away. So not lingering, not hurrying, I crossed the flood."

I love this example for its sense of great delicacy, of ease, of naturalness. Not lingering, not sinking, not drowning, and also not hurrying, not pushing forward in a hasty or stressful manner because of too much expectation. To understand this beautiful balance, we need to understand what acceptance means.

Acceptance doesn't mean succumbing to what's going on. When we succumb to a situation, we collapse into it or become immersed in it or possessed by it. While trying to cross the flood, instead of moving, we linger and we drown, we get possessed by the waves of the flood, we are overcome by them. Yet acceptance clearly doesn't mean we struggle against the waves. Trying to push against the waves or push them out of the way exhausts us and is futile. We have to use the momentum of each wave on the crossing to help us go along. But it takes a special kind of strength to be able to be this delicate, to be able to be in the middle of the flood, not sinking and not thrashing around.

The crossing of the flood is only accomplished one moment at a time. The art of this accomplishment is the ability to continually begin again. This is the other side of letting go, the doorway letting go reveals. We set forth, we struggle or get muddled or anxious, we lose our balance, and then realizing it, we begin again. We don't need self-recriminations or blame or anger. We need a reawakening of intention and a willingness to recommit, to be wholehearted once again.

Beginning again is the consummate act of practicing equanimity.

Living and working with wisdom and compassion is a combination of accepting what arises before us as conditioned, therefore not subject to our singular willful control, and also seeing it as changing constantly, therefore always suggestive of possibility.

The philosopher Søren Kierkegaard expressed these two poles as the necessary and the possible. To reframe that in the language of Buddhist psychology, the *necessary* points to what we find in the moment, including the immense number of conditions that brought us here: our heritage and background and the decisions we've made. And it's all that we see before us, the presentation of the universe as it is configured in this moment.

The *possible* is the expansive aspect, the inevitability of change: nothing is static, fixed, the world is continually being reborn, and we as part of it. We can thus envision, aspire, and transform.

To be present—alive and effective—we try to live a life with a sense of both necessity *and* possibility. There has to be a balance. If there's all necessity and no possibility, one is trapped in the world of present conditions, resigned to how it all appears to be, without a vision of how it could be.

If it's all possibility and no necessity, one is trapped in idealistic fantasy, overlooking the actual conditions of the moment, which are the basis for authentic change and transformation.

With the one extreme, we despair due to lack of inspiration. With the other extreme, we despair because we've forgotten to incorporate and accept what presently is—the acknowledgment of which is an essential component of the way our dreams come true.

We can be encouraged by the power of our intentions, renewed by our ability to begin again, and continually supported by the dynamic relationship of the two.

DO WHAT YOU CAN DO WITH WHAT'S IN FRONT OF YOU

MY COLLEAGUE MARK Coleman, who often teaches retreats in the wilderness and is the author of *Awake in the Wild,* wrote in *Mindful* magazine:

Mindfulness teachings point us to meet the present moment as it is: We behold both the beauty of nature and the devastation that is occurring. We see the folly of overly romanticizing the past or drowning in doomsday scenarios of what's to come . . . In learning the power of inclining our mind, we can also turn our attention to the tremendous number of constructive solutions that millions of people around the planet are working on. Organizations around the world are figuring out how to remove plastics from the ocean, draw carbon from the air, restore habitat for tigers in Nepal, and clean up the Ganges River. . . . These times require our mindfulness practice to hold a wide view. They ask that we hold the harsh reality of the eco-crisis, the beauty of what is still here and thriving, and simultaneously the uprising of ordinary people working all over the planet to steward, protect, and preserve the earth in sustainable ways. I have walked through scorched forests. I can look at the blackened trunks and feel a tender grief. And I can also focus on the emerald green shoots that rise out of the ashes. Both are true. Both demand our attention. To be awake today is to learn how to hold paradox in your mind and to dwell in ambiguity.

MEASURING GOOD

RECENTLY, I TAUGHT a meditation workshop at a large nonprofit foundation that does good work all around the world. As I prepared to teach one day, I looked past the staff facing me and saw a giant sign on the wall in the back. It read, "If you can't measure it, it didn't happen."

Of course, in the world of philanthropy, it's understandable that the goal would be to actually ease suffering, not just talk about doing so while wasting money and time—embittering those involved as hope turns to weariness, and weariness to a sense of defeat. Being able to measure the "results" of good work therefore becomes a metric for trying to understand goodness.

When we are trying to assess the value of our actions in everyday life, we typically do so in terms of expectations. Did we do the good thing we envisioned in the time frame we anticipated? While self-awareness and setting goals is a powerful practice, becoming too rigid about achieving results can lead to a relentless kind of expectation. Then burnout can result, likely with a desolating habit of feeling we can never do enough.

We may, through force of habit, disparage ourselves by considering our actions to be inadequate or resign ourselves to their seeming mediocrity, but we can't possibly know the ultimate result of what we do. As the poet T. S. Eliot wrote, "For us there is only the trying. The rest is not our business." This larger vision of life is what sustains our efforts to bring about change, beyond the immediate success or failure of a given action.

In Buddhist teaching, the immediate result of an action is only a part of its value. There are two other significant aspects: the intention giving rise to an action and the skillfulness with which we perform it. The intention is our basic motivation, or the inner urge that sparks the action. As the Dalai Lama has said, "Motivation is very important, and thus my simple religion is love, respect for others, honesty: teachings that cover not only religion but also the fields of politics, economics, business, science, law, medicine—everywhere. With proper motivation these can help humanity."

That is the core of our commitments and values coming to life in our choices, our direction, our decisions. An action can be motivated by love—or by hatred and revenge. Self-interest can be the source of what we do—or generosity can. So first knowing, and then refining, our intentions—the place from which we act—becomes a large area of inner work.

SKILLFUL ACTION

THE SKILLFULNESS WITH which we act relies on carrying out our intention with sensitivity to and awareness of what might be appropriate to any given situation. This is the discernment we talked about in the previous chapter. In aligning intention and skillfulness, we challenge assumptions, stretch to new ways of thinking and acting.

How to act skillfully is contingent on context. In some situations, our discernment, our best sense of how to act, leads us to say a resounding "No," and set the boundaries we need. In other situations, our discernment leads us to say, emphatically, "Yes."

This also leads to the question of cultural competency. To rely solely on the goodness of one's intention without looking at the impact of what we are doing or saying, particularly in a context of diverse backgrounds or experiences, is to have only a partial understanding of our action. We need to hold that bigger view we talked about in the previous chapter, to know as best we can the context in which our action will emerge.

Let's go back to Mark Coleman's quotation: "To be awake today is to learn how to hold paradox in your mind and to dwell in ambiguity." In deciding skillful action, we need this wider view and an opening to bigger possibilities revealed by systems thinking, along with a fine-grained focus on easing the suffering of the person just in front of us.

CHANGE THE LENS

WE CAN SO easily get lost in massive numbers—"this many refugees, this much disruption"—and then disparage any effort to do the good in front of us because it seems too small. It's important to keep track of the vastness of an issue, but working to try to change things for one person, or one set of people, isn't nothing. Working to try to change things for one animal isn't nothing. We need a great big vision of change and also a commitment to improving the life of even just one. There is a famous story by the anthropologist Loren Eiseley that illustrates just this:

One day a man was walking along the beach, when he noticed a boy hurriedly picking up and gently throwing things into the ocean.

Approaching the boy, he asked, "Young man, what are you doing?"

The boy replied, "Throwing starfish back into the ocean. The surf is up and the tide is going out. If I don't throw them back, they'll die."

The man laughed to himself and said, "Don't you realize there are miles and miles of beach and hundreds of starfish? You can't make any difference!"

After listening politely, the boy bent down, picked up another starfish, and threw it into the surf. Then, smiling at the man, he said,

"I made a difference to that one."

IF YOU EDUCATE a child and the resultant benefit to society doesn't show for twenty years, how does that tally with being able to measure a result? If we plant a seed and can't determine the exact time that seed will blossom, don't we consider how we planted it, nurturing the soil and protecting the growth, as having done the best we can?

We do what we do fully, wholeheartedly, and completely because of our sense of urgency at the suffering we witness, yet we need to do it without panic, without a rush to judgment, because the unfolding will happen in its own way, at its own speed. If our dedicated intention is toward goodness, toward being whole in our actions, then that will be the thread that will lead us on. We do what we need to do, one step at a time, with confidence and joy, and let it unfold. I think that's about the best advice we could get.

I used to look back at people in the civil rights movement in the United States, or the women's suffrage movement, or the labor movement, and think, *Wow, isn't it amazing? They were so brave, they went out, and did these incredibly courageous things and risked being stigmatized, or getting beaten up. Or killed. But they knew it's what they had to do to win.* And then I realized one day, *They didn't know they were going to win.*

That's the arrogance of history. We look back and think, *Of course, this is what they had to do. They knew this is what they had to do to get this done.* But they didn't know they were going to get it done, because in fact, we don't know. In the moment, we're always entering that unknown. And we do what we do, because it's what we feel we need to do. But that is quite a task. So we keep connecting to something that will energize us and keep us going—our values, a vision of life as it might look, those who have come before us, and one another.

I was startled to discover that a single redwood tree, after it falls, contributes to the ecosystem for three hundred to four hundred years, five times longer than it was alive. Its trunk, limbs, and roots become food for other species in the forest. The stump of the fallen tree raises a new seedling above the forest floor to receive sunlight so it can grow. Eventually, the roots of the new tree grow around the stump to reach the ground.

Using nature as an example, picture the impact of an activist extending for three or four hundred years after their lifetime. I think of the influence of Mahatma Gandhi on theologian and educator Dr. Howard Thurman, promoting the power of non-violent resistance when he visited him in India. Dr. Thurman served as a spiritual advisor to many towering figures in the U.S. civil rights movement, including Dr. Martin Luther King Jr., who was a driving inspiration for me and for countless people of this time—and I'm sure into the future.

In the meditation tradition, we call this profound connection to those who came before us and helped mold us *lineage*. A sense of lineage is another way we let go of self-preoccupation and realize we are a part of a larger fabric of life. It is a way to find the energy to try to affect the world while also recognizing we are not in control. This brings us to much greater balance.

When I am teaching, for example, I'm not sitting there thinking, *I'm influencing the world!* or *Saving this person is my personal burden to carry!* I'm just doing my best to help those in front of me at that moment.

I recently had a conversation about this with Barry Boyce, a meditation teacher and the founding editor of *Mindful* magazine.

He commented, "When I'm teaching, it's always helpful to remember that it's not all about me. I am a small part of a very big picture. I'm coming out of a lineage of people who taught me, who were taught by others, stretching very far back. I'm just the vessel through which someone can receive what I've learned, however incomplete, and we can learn together in the moment as a result."

Some sense of connection to something larger than ourselves, whether it's a lineage or a present-day community, takes away pressure to have a singular, special achievement and be the savior of the world. Equanimity is cultivated by the sincere effort to do our best, coupled with the realization that "it's not all about me."

BE PRESENT

THE ESSENTIAL SPIRIT of activism, as in meditation, or service, or love, is showing up in connection and compassion and without self-importance. Buddhist monk Thich Nhat Hanh—who is associated perhaps more than any other figure with the term *engaged Buddhism*—has written how "the most precious gift we can offer others is our presence."

Joanna Macy echoes this: "I'm not insisting that we be brimming with hope. It's OK not to be optimistic. Buddhist teachings say feeling that you have to maintain hope can wear you out. So just be present. The biggest gift you can give is to be absolutely present. And when you're worrying about whether you're hopeful or hopeless or pessimistic or optimistic, who cares? The main thing is that you're showing up, that you're here, and that you're finding ever more capacity to love this world because it will not be healed without that."

Joshin talks about his relationship with his dad in a way that exemplifies this extraordinary gift of just showing up:

Late in life, my father had come off the streets, and one of my sisters started to take care of him. He was still an alcoholic, but now he had been diagnosed with esophageal cancer. Even though he had smoked six packs of cigarettes a day for the last seventy years and drank twenty-four cans of beer a day, he was shocked. When they told him all they could do was make him comfortable for a few months, he asked if I would visit him. Even though my first reaction was, "Really? Do I have to do this?" I decided I should go.

He was living in one little room that smelled of cigarette smoke. He was drawn out, skinny, not well. And he said to me, "You know, they told me I'm dying."

I said, "I heard that."

He said, "So I wanted to see you."

Then he got quiet, so I decided I would just sit there quietly, as well. For the next three days, every now and then, the silence would be broken by a story about his life. He was telling me stories about failure or stories where he hurt someone. They were dark stories, stories where he had gotten lost or he felt like he didn't live up to his obligations. He detailed his regrets and mistakes, the wrong turns in his life. He told me a story about being homeless in New York and getting a job as a dishwasher at a hotel in Times Square. One day, they called him off the dishwasher line and asked him to make sandwiches, and he did pretty well. And then one day, the head sandwich maker didn't show up for work, so they said to my father, "Ed, can you make the sandwiches today for the executive team?" And my father jumped on it, and the people liked his work. Next day, they said, "Ed, we'd like to give you this new job of making sandwiches for the executives."

My father told me, "Ah, I was so excited about it. That was a great thing!"

Then he went back to the shelter he was living in, and he got really nervous. He thought, *I can't do this. I'm just going to fuck it up.* He decided not to go back to work. This was a big regret for him, a missed opportunity.

My heart broke. I thought, *My father felt inadequate to make sandwiches.* I saw the depth of his pain. I realized he was going to confession. We'd sit on the sofa and he would look straight ahead as if we were in a confessional. And I'd just listen. Just bearing witness.

This is where my practice really helped me. I could see my resentment and anger, my rage and blame coming up, but I knew I didn't have to pursue it. I found myself more capable than ever to just be with him as he is. Feeling that, he continued to reveal more and more of his life, his regrets. I realized, though, that if this is confession, there will need to be absolution—to show him he's forgiven. I tried to say some words to make him feel better, but they sounded like platitudes: "We all make mistakes."

I decided to cook him a meal, one my mother used to make, an Italian meal he loved. I made a tomato sauce from scratch, some vegetables he loved, and pasta. I put the meal on the table and poured him a glass of wine. My siblings were all there at this feast. He ate that food like he was in heaven. He glowed with pleasure. He wept at the table. I think he felt forgiven.

This shifted something in me. I felt like I reclaimed some part of my life and he reclaimed some part of his life. And we did that together.

I have been in a number of rooms like that, literally and figuratively—sitting with someone who doesn't quite know how to live in this world, who feels apart or has been set apart, who has been badly hurt and sometimes has hurt others badly. Rooms marked by abandonment and despair.

It takes a lot to enter a room like that and sit there awhile. Watching your reactions, your resentments and fears come and go, not rushing to deny what you are witnessing and also not rushing to try to fix it (if it even can be fixed). It takes a lot, certainly, if it is your own father and your own history playing out, but it takes a lot no matter what the circumstances.

I've found that it takes strength and also a willingness to move away from a cozy, comfortable place of avoidance. It takes fortitude and a real caring for others. And it takes an ability to step out of the way so that your own ego gratification isn't occupying center stage. It takes an ability to sit there in wholehearted presence and be resourceful enough to recognize that sometimes the best thing you can do is strategize about resolving someone's pain, and sometimes the best thing you can do is let go of that strategizing and just make them a glorious meal—because they are worth it, even if they themselves somehow forgot that half a lifetime ago.

Joshin's story made me think of my own father and all his difficulties and our difficulties together. But not just of him. All around the world, there are so many struggling people, and it's easy to feel overwhelmed and helpless facing that reality. I want the trajectory of my own life, though, to be one where I don't avoid the suffering of others but I work to be present, and openhearted, and caring, while caring for myself as well.

I want to connect in love to not just the suffering but also the strength and beauty of others. I want to connect as skillfully as I can, with wisdom and discernment. I know that to do that in an ongoing way, I need to keep cultivating awareness and balance. Every day.

I've learned that the path of connecting in hard places is made a lot easier by the company of others who are also trying. I've learned that giving goes both ways and that those who largely dwell in those rooms can have a lot to offer those who largely enjoy more freedom. I've learned that, just like water, compassion is strong, soft, and immensely powerful. Most essentially, I've learned that to continue to be worthwhile to myself and others, I need to be revitalized by finding a place of peace, over and over again. From this place of peace, from the radiant calm of equanimity, many good things will grow.

PRACTICE: CULTIVATING EQUANIMITY

I WAS ONCE speaking to a group of people and said, "I think that if I was in charge of the universe, it would be a lot better world." Someone in the group called out, "Are you sure?" I considered that for a moment then firmly replied, "I am really sure!" But alas, one of the great poignancies in life is that we're not ultimately in control. Because of that, what we are looking for is the balance between compassion and equanimity. Compassion can be thought of as the heart's moving toward suffering to see if we can be of help. Equanimity is a spacious stillness that can accept things as they are. The balance of compassion and equanimity allows us to care and yet not get overwhelmed and unable to cope because of that caring.

The phrases we use reflect this balance. Choose one or two phrases that are personally meaningful to you. There are some options offered below. You can alter them in any way or use others that you create.

To begin the practice, take as comfortable a position as possible, sitting or lying down. Take a few deep, soft breaths to let your body settle. Bring your attention to your breath to begin with. When you feel ready you can switch your attention to the silent repetition of the phrases you've chosen. Begin to silently say your chosen phrases over and over again.

Feel the meaning of what you are saying, yet without trying to force anything. Let the practice carry you along. You can call a particular person to mind—get an image of them or say their name to yourself, get a feeling for their presence, and see what happens as you silently repeat the phrases you've chosen, such as:

I care about your pain yet cannot control it.

I will care for you and cannot keep you from suffering.

May I offer love, knowing I can't control the course of life, suffering, or death.

I wish you happiness and peace yet cannot make your choices for you.

And then move on to consider the boundlessness of life—people, creatures—as you silently repeat one or two phrases that express our capacity to connect to and care for all of life and also know peace:

I will work to alleviate suffering in this world, and I know I'm not in control of the unfolding of the universe.

May I recognize my limits compassionately, just as I recognize the limitations of others.

May I remember compassion as I work to be undisturbed by the comings and goings of events.

When you feel ready, you can open your eyes. See if you can bring some of this sense of spaciousness and compassion into your day.

GRATEFUL
ACKNOWLEDGMENTS

✳

I am inspired every day by the many people who work hard to advocate for those who are easily abandoned or overlooked. They enrich all of our lives.

I am grateful to everyone who agreed to be interviewed for or included in this book. Whether or not someone is directly quoted here, every single person I reached out to helped guide my vision and establish my priorities in writing. Charlotte Lieberman and Sara Overton skillfully conducted the interviews.

Joy Harris, my literary agent, has always been my champion. Bob Miller of Flatiron Books has been a continual source of encouragement.

Barry Boyce, who worked as a developmental editor on this manuscript, created clear style and structure for all my varied attempts at saying what I cared about. Lise Funderburg led me to go far deeper in learning writing as a craft, which is something I've always wanted.

Writing this book coincided with a time of my healing from an illness, when I have been supported emotionally, financially, and practically by a group of wonderful friends. I could never have written this book or recovered so well without them.

INDEX

✳

AA. *See* Alcoholics Anonymous
Abbey of Gethsemani, 96–97
ACT UP. *See* AIDS Coalition to Unleash
   Power
activism. *See also specific activists; specific*
   organizations
AIDS, 63
   environmental, 176–77, 179, 209–10
   fast-food worker, 24, 40, 112
   gun violence, 14, 34–35, 39, 112–13
   lineage, 214–15
   marriage equality, 69–70, 73–74
   music for, 118–19, 198–99
   poverty, 176–78
   power from, 38–39
   slavery, modern, 61, 178
   sparks of, 138–42
   violence against women, 56–57
activist burnout, 113, 114–15
addiction
   AA for, 57, 59–60
   meditation for, 98, 121
   opioid, 99–100
   Recovery Café helping battle, 48–50
   root of, 109–10
agency, ix, 10
   definition and role of, 36, 37
   forces beyond our control impacting,
      45–47
   non-exclusion from, 48–50
   transition toward, 38–39
agents of change, 40
Agler, Ellen, 94, 130–31, 186–87
AIDS Coalition to Unleash Power
   (ACT UP), 63

AIDS crisis, 61–63
Alcoholics Anonymous (AA), 57,
   59–60
Allison, Dorothy, 38, 162–63
amyotrophic lateral sclerosis (ALS), 33–34,
   116–17
Angelou, Maya, 64
anger, ix
   cost of, 56–60
   energy of, harnessing the, 69–71
   honoring the message of, 63–66
   mindfulness of, 66–67
   movement beyond, 60–63
   perspective on, broadening, 71–75
   power of, harnessing the, 67–69
   usefulness of, 54–56
apartheid, 45
art
   benevolent contagion and, 122
   empathy building from, 164–65
   as radical practice, 18–19
   suffering in relation to, 90–92
Arts & Understanding, 62–63
asylum-seeking, 22–23
authenticity, 131–34
awakening
   of energy, 53–54
   joy, 116–22
awareness
   of death, 71–72
   of embodied self, 191–92
   environmental, 176–77, 179, 209–10
   of interconnectedness, 2–3
   of suffering, 93–94
   of thoughts, 51–52

Bajacu' Boricua, 18–19
Baldwin, James, 60, 202, 203
Banaji, Mahzarin, 170–71
Barkan, Ady, 33–34, 116–17
Bastard Out of Carolina (Allison), 38, 162–63
Bateson, Gregory, 12
Be More America, 95
Begley, Sharon, 152
bell hooks Institute, 43–45
benevolent contagion, 122
Bergman, Ingrid, 12
bias
    attribution, 172–73
    mindfulness of, 173–75
    riddle on, 170–71
    tendency toward, 169
black people, 33, 44–45, 119
Bodhi, Bhikkhu, 21, 177–78
Boorstein, Sylvia, 93
Boyce, Barry, 215–16
breath
    attention on, 51, 90, 103
    gathering our energy and, 27–29
Brewer, Jud, 154–56
Brooklyn, 24, 197–98
Buddha, 57
    on eight worldly winds, 203–4
    inspiration from, 1, 4–5
    on justice, fairness, and generosity, 176
    on suffering, 79, 104, 207
Buddhism
    adjustments in applying, 21
    on anger, 58, 60, 65
    gladdening the mind technique of, 119–20
Buddhist Global Relief, 177–78
Burks, Ruth Coker, 62–63

Capehart, Jonathan, 119
care
    choosing to, 33–34
    self, 113–16, 142
Caring Across Generations, 36–37
Cash, Rosanne, 18
Catholicism, 197–98
Center for Green Schools, 115, 152–53
Center for Investigating Healthy Minds,
    127–28
Center for Transformative Change, 113–14
Chanthawong, Eakapol, 15
CHASRS. *See* Chicago Health, Aging, and
    Social Relation Study
Chavez, Cesar, 55
Chavkin, Rachel, 163
Chemaly, Soraya, 54
Chen, Cher Weixia, 114–15

Chicago Health, Aging, and Social Relation
    Study (CHASRS), 150
Cleveland, Ohio, 16, 142–43
Cleveland Clinic, 142–43
Coleman, Mark, 209–10, 212
colonialism, 73, 187
compassion, ix
    anger defeated with, 61
    corps, 159–61
    empathy compared to, 128–31
    equanimity and, 205–6, 220–22
    fighting and, 161–63
    from meditation, 179–81
    understanding of interconnection and,
        158
    visualization on living with, 2
conformity, 131–34
contraction and expansion, 154–56
courage, ix, 75, 91–92
COVID-19, vii–ix
creativity, 90–92
Crow, Jenna, 49–50
Cutler, Ken, 35
Cutler, Sharon, 34–35

Dalai Lama, 96
    on art, 91
    on love from a distance, 159
    meditation study participation, 127–28
    on motivation, 211
    on 9/11, 87
Daniels, Joel, 89–90, 103, 117
Dass, Ram, 131–33
Daumal, René, 124–25
Davidson, Richie, 126–27
Davis, Susan, 58–59, 112
Davis, Viola, 40
death, 71–72
DeChristopher, Tim, 159–61
Democratic Republic of the Congo, 85, 120
depression, 125–26
DeSteno, David, 179–80, 186
disenfranchisement, 32, 46, 124
Doering, Sarah, 25
double bind theory, 12
Dutt, Mallika, 56–57, 139–41, 147, 164

Eggers, Dave, 32
Einstein, Albert, 190
Eiseley, Loren, 213
Eliot, T. S., 211
Emory University, 90–91
emotions. *See also* anger; fear; grief; joy
    being with difficult thoughts and, 75–78
    equanimity of, 195–96

empathy
  art for building, 164–65
  Cleveland Clinic video on, 142–43
  compassion compared to, 128–31
  disconnection from, 143–44
  excellence, engagement, and, 144–45
END Fund, 94, 130–31, 186–87
energy
  of anger, harnessing the, 69–71
  awakening of, 53–54
  loss of, 84–85
  placement of, 50
  practice of gathering our, 27–29
environmental awareness/activism, 176–77,
  179, 209–10
equanimity
  actions taken with, 206–7
  for crossing the flood of suffering, 207–9
  defining, 193–94
  development of, 203–6
  of emotions, 195–96
  power of, 200–202
  practice of cultivating, 220–22
  representation of, 196–200
expansion and contraction, 154–56

Fast Food Forward, 24
Fast Food Justice, 24
fast-food workers, 24, 40, 112
fatigue, 128–31
fear
  grip of, 41–42
  loneliness from, 10–11
Fences, 40
Fischer, Norman, 96–97
Fisher, Carrie, 57
Fitzgerald, Emmett, 85–87
Flamboyan Arts Fund, 18–19
Ford, Erica, 189–90
forgiveness, 160–61, 218–19
Frazier, Ken, 45
Fredrickson, Barbara, 58
Freedom Fund, 178
Freeman, Jonathan, 152

Gadsby, Hannah, 92
Gandhi, Mahatma, 57, 215
Ganz, Marshall, 55
Garrison Institute, 100–102, 110, 194–95
gaslighting, 12
George Mason University School of
  Integrative Studies, 114–15
gladdening the mind technique,
  119–20
Goldstein, Joseph, 25–26, 41, 123

González, Andrés, 65, 125, 196. *See also*
  Holistic Life Foundation
goodness, measuring, 210–12
Google, 12, 13, 57
Gorski, Paul C., 114–15
Green Belt Movement, 176–77
Greenpeace, 38–39
grief. *See also* pain/suffering
  defining, 81
  freedom to express, 82–83
guilt, 114–15, 160, 201
Gupta, Anurag, 95, 153–54, 172, 207
Guttenberg, Fred, 98–99
Gutter, Rachel, 115, 152–53, 206–7

Hadestown, 163
Halifax, Joan, 88, 137–38
Hanh, Thich Nhat, 139, 146–47, 216
Havel, Václav, 103
health issues
  of loneliness, 149–51
  of violence, 189–90
Hernández, Daisy, 203, 204–5
Highlander Folk School/Research and
  Education Center, 83–84, 111
Hiroshima (Japan), vii–viii
Holistic Life Foundation (HLF), 18
  after-school program, 196
  on anger, 65–66
  motto of, 181
  self-care taught at, 142
Holocaust, 72
homelessness
  Recovery Café helping battle, 48–50
  reflection on, 137–38, 217–18
hooks, bell
  Institute, 43–45
  on love, 26
  on social action, 17–18
Horton, Myles, 83–84, 111
Hurricane Andrew, 204–5
Hurricane Maria, 18–19

ICE detention centers, 23
identity
  intersectionality in relation to, 139–41
  lovingkindness practice regarding,
    191–92
  stories influencing, 43–45
India, 16, 43, 56
Insight Meditation Society (IMS)
  PTSD at, 81–82
  retreat, 123
  story of belonging at, 44
  vision for, 25–26

institutionalization, 46
intentions, 211–12
interconnectedness
    awareness of, 2–3
    intersectionality leading to, 139–41,
        164
    living with vision of, 163–65
    love from, 26–27
    movement toward, 156–59
    network looking for, 181–83
    teamwork and, 147–49
intersectionality, 139–41, 164
Iowa, 163–64
Iraq, 81, 118
Israel, 38

Jamail, Dahr, 83
Japan, 151
Jerusalem, 72
Jeste, Dilip, 151
Jim Crow laws, 84
Jones, Sarah, 19, 117, 122
joy, ix
    awakening, 116–22
    desire for, 109–10
    practice of cultivating, 134–36
    refusal of, 125–26
Judt, Tony, 18

Kaiser Family Foundation, 150–51
Kaufman, Sari, 14
King, Martin Luther, Jr., 157, 215
Kink, Michael, 97–98
Klimecki, Olga, 128
Kornfield, Jack, 25–26, 123
Krukiel, May, 100–101
Kumanyika, Chenjerai, 84

Latinx, 33
Lazarus, Emma, 31
LGBTQ people, 70
LIFE Camp, 189–90
loneliness
    fear causing, 10–11
    meditation and, 149–51
    pain in relation to, 103–4
love, ix
    from a distance, 159
    from interconnectedness, 26–27
    light, darkness and, 120
    self, 117
lovingkindness practice, viii–ix
    for embodied self, 191–92
    for ourselves and others,
        165–68

toward ourselves, 104–8
    role of, 9–10, 20–22
Luagoviña, Francisco Genkoji ("Paco"),
    70–71, 72, 99–100

Maathai, Wangari, 176–77
Macy, Joanna, 201–2, 204, 216
Magee, Rhonda, 185, 186
Mandela, Nelson, 57
Mann, Sam, 183–84, 186
March for Our Lives, 14, 34–35
Marjory Stoneman Douglas High School.
    See Parkland, Florida
marriage equality, 69–70, 73–74
mass shootings, 14, 34–35, 39, 89, 98–99,
    112–13, 201
Maxson, Rose Lee, 40
McCourt, Malachy, 57
meditation, viii
    for addiction, 98, 121
    benefits of, 21–22, 93–94
    compassion from, 179–81
    contemplation prior to, 7–8
    experimentation with, 4
    in India, studying, 43
    lineage, 215–16
    loneliness and, 149–51
    perspective from, 3
    as social practice, 1–2
    study on pain and, 126–28
    as transportable tranquility, 15
Merck, 45
Merck, Friedrike, 121
Merton, Thomas, 96
#mettaminute, 22–24
Miami University, Ohio, 203
Mindful magazine, 13, 113, 152, 209–10,
    215
mindfulness
    of anger, 66–67
    of bias, 173–75
    clear comprehension and, 184–85
    role of, 9–10, 20–22
    teachers, 38–39, 86–87, 112–13, 147–49
Miranda, Lin-Manuel, 18–19, 50, 72
misogyny, 13
Moayed, Arian, 144
Moyers, Bill, 118–19
Mumford, George, 147–49
Murthy, Vivek, 150

National Basketball Association, 148
National Domestic Workers Alliance,
    36–37
network looking, 181–83

New York City, 24, 63, 197–98
  LIFE Camp in, 189–90
  9/11 in, 87
  Statue of Liberty in, 30–32, 41
  subway visualization, 2
New York Times, 13, 45, 74
New York University, 152
Nichtern, Ethan, 159
9/11, 87
Nobel Peace Prize, 61, 177
Noe, Killian, 48–49
Noguera, Pedro, 143–44
North African ethnicity, 73
North Star, 12–13, 75
Northeastern University, 179–80
Notes of a Native Son (Baldwin), 202, 203
Nottage, Lynn, 19, 88, 91, 120, 164–65
Novick, Samantha, 34–35, 89, 201

opioid epidemic, 99–100
Orthodox Jewish family, 38
Owens, Lama Rod, 60

pain/suffering, vii–ix
  avoiding extremes of, 92–95
  Buddha on, 79, 104, 207
  creativity and, 90–92
  crossing the flood of, 207–9
  gentleness with, 122–25
  intimacy of, 97–100
  loneliness in relation to, 103–4
  meditation study regarding, 126–28
  recognition and acknowledgment of,
    80–83, 87–88
  root of, 96–97
  sculpting the, 100–103
Pandita, Sayadaw U, 123
Papa John's Pizza, 24
Parkland, Florida, 14, 34–35, 39, 89, 98–99,
    112–13, 201
Parkland City Commission, 35
A People's History of the United States (Zinn), 50
perspective
  on anger, broadening, 71–75
  from meditation, 3
  reality and, 185–87
PETA, 38–39
Poo, Ai-Jen, 36–37
post-traumatic stress disorder (PTSD), 49,
    80, 81–82
poverty
  environmental depletion in relation to,
    176–77
  self-worth impacted by, 46, 47
  understanding roots of, 177–78

power
  from activism, 38–39
  of anger, harnessing the, 67–69
  anger transforming into, 61
  of equanimity, 200–202
  of love, 26–27
  rediscovery of, 49–50
  water contemplation for summoning,
    15–16
presence, 216–20
PTSD. *See* post-traumatic stress disorder
Puerto Rico, 18–19, 71
purpose, sense of, 34–37

racism, 153–54, 163–64, 183–84
radical acts, 19, 40
radical practice, 16–19
radical thinking, 18
Ralph Bunche Plaza, 71
Reagon, Bernice Johnson, 118–19, 198–99
reconciliation, 159
Recovery Café, 48–50
resentment, 59–60
resilience
  building, 88–90
  of human spirit, 116
  insight into, 12–13
  need for, 83–87
Ricard, Matthieu, 127–28
Rilke, Rainer Maria, 103

Salbi, Zainab, 118
Sales, Ruby, 119
salvation, 42–43
sampajanna, 184
sati, 184
Satyarthi, Kailash, 61
schizophrenia, 12
Schrijver, Iris, 111–12
Schrijver, Karel, 111–12
Seattle, 48–50
self, embodied, 191–92
self-care
  HLF teaching, 142
  Mindful magazine on, 113
  self-indulgence compared to, 113–14
  support for, lack of, 114–16
self-exploration, 69–70
self-love, 117
self-protection, 54
self-worth
  anger as assertion of, 55
  elevation of, 48–49
  poverty impacting, 46, 47
  punishment of, 39–40

sex trade, 175–76
sexual abuse/assault, 40, 49
shame, 114–15, 160
shock of witnessing, 80
Silver, Diane, 11
Singer, Tania, 128
Sivaraksa, Sulak, 175–76, 186
skillful action, 212–13
slavery, modern, 61, 178
Smith, Ali, 65–66, 125. *See also* Holistic
    Life Foundation
Smith, Atman, 65, 125, 142. *See also* Holistic
    Life Foundation
Smith, Rodney, 82
social action, 17–18, 91. *See also* activism
Solnit, Rebecca, 179
Solomon, Marc, 69–70, 73–74
Solutions Journalism, 13
spectrum of depletion, 85
Statue of Liberty, 30–32, 41
stories. *See also specific stories*
    exploration of our, 51–52
    identity influenced by, 43–45
    negative and positive news, 13
stress relief patterns, 110–14
stress response, 8–10
Student Nonviolent Coordinating
    Committee, 118–19
suffering. *See* pain/suffering
survivor guilt, 201
system entrepreneur, 187–88
systems change approach, 178–81

teamwork, 147–49
Thoreau, Henry David, 142
thoughts
    awareness of, 51–52
    being with difficult emotions and,
    75–78
Thurman, Howard, 215
Thurman, Robert, 2
Tibbetts, Rob, 163–64
Tippett, Krista, 170–71, 201–2
tranquility, transportable, 15
tree contemplation, 145–47
Truthout, 83
Tutu, Desmond, 99
Twain, Mark, 57

Twitter
    #mettaminute on, 22–24
    Solutions Journalism on, 13
Tygielski, Shelly, 38–39, 112–13

UCLA, 143–44
United Nations, 71
United States
    AIDS crisis in, 61–63
    border, 22–23
    culture of disconnection in, 143–44
University of Maryland, 65
University of North Carolina at Chapel
    Hill, 58
Upaya Zen Center, 137–38
upekkha, 193–94
Upworthy, 13

Van Gogh, Vincent, 92
Vexler, Dan, 178
vicarious trauma exercise, 100–102
violence
    as public health issue, 189–90
    against women, 56–57

Walker, Shantel, 24, 40, 112
Washington Post, 13, 119
water
    contemplation on, 15–16
    love in relation to, 27
Waterwell, 144
widow's walk, 42
williams, angel Kyodo, 113–14
Wisdom 2.0, 98–99
Wolfson, Evan, 74
Women for Women International, 118
Women's Leadership Center at Omega
    Institute, 139
World War II, 18
Wright, Robert, 172–73

Yad Vashem, 72
Yale University, 18
You Got to Move, 84
Yountz, Heather, 67–68
youth arts, 18–19

Zinn, Howard, 50